THE STRUCTURE OF VIOLENCE

Armed Forces as
Social Systems

SAGE SERIES ON ARMED FORCES AND SOCIETY

INTER-UNIVERSITY SEMINAR ON ARMED FORCES AND SOCIETY

Morris Janowitz, *University of Chicago*
Chairman and Series Editor

Charles C. Moskos, Jr., *Northwestern University*
Associate Chairman and Series Editor

Also in this series:

Vol. I   HANDBOOK OF MILITARY INSTITUTIONS
          Edited by Roger W. Little

Vol. II   MILITARY PROFESSIONALIZATION AND POLITICAL POWER
          by Bengt Abrahamson

Vol. III MILITARY INSTITUTIONS AND THE SOCIOLOGY OF WAR:
          A Review of the Literature with Annotated Bibliography
          by Kurt Lang

Vol. IV   THE UNITED STATES ARMY IN TRANSITION
          by Zeb B. Bradford, Jr. and Frederic J. Brown

Vol. V   SOLDIERS AND KINSMEN IN UGANDA:
          The Making of a Military Ethnocracy
          by Ali A. Mazrui

Vol. VI   SOCIOLOGY AND THE MILITARY ESTABLISHMENT:
          Third Edition
          by Morris Janowitz
          in collaboration with
          Roger W. Little

Vol. VII THE SOLDIER AND SOCIAL CHANGE:
          Comparative Studies in the History and Sociology of the Military
          by Jacques van Doorn

Vol. VIII MILITARY ROLES IN MODERNIZATION
          Civil-Military Relations in Thailand and Burma
          by Moshe Lissak

Vol. IX   FAMILIES IN THE MILITARY SYSTEM
          **Edited by Hamilton I. McCubbin, Barbara B. Dahl,
          and Edna J. Hunter**

Vol. X   THE STRUCTURE OF VIOLENCE
          by Maury D. Feld

Vol. XI   THE GENESIS OF THE PROFESSIONAL OFFICERS' CORPS
          by G. Teitler

Vol. XII THE LIMITS OF MILITARY INTERVENTION
          Edited by Ellen Stern

THE STRUCTURE

OF VIOLENCE

Armed Forces as
Social Systems

Maury D. Feld

Harvard University

Preface by

Charles C. Moskos, Jr.

WITHDRAWN

SAGE PUBLICATIONS   Beverly Hills / London

For information address:

SAGE PUBLICATIONS, INC.
275 South Beverly Drive
Beverly Hills, California 90212

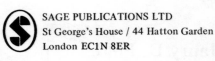

SAGE PUBLICATIONS LTD
St George's House / 44 Hatton Garden
London EC1N 8ER

Printed in the United States of America

Library of Congress Cataloging in Publication Data

Feld, Maury D.
      The structure of violence

      (Sage series on armed forces and society; 10)
         1. Sociology, Military.   2. Armed Forces.
I. Title.
U21.5.F44   301.5'93   76-50503
ISBN O-3039-0729-X

FIRST PRINTING

CONTENTS

PREFACE by Charles C. Moskos, Jr.   9

ACKNOWLEDGEMENTS   11

CHAPTERS

1   Military Discipline as a Social Force   13

2   A Typology of Military Organization   31

3   Information and Authority: The Structure of
     Military Organization   71

4   The Military Self-Image in a Technological
     Environment   85

5   Professionalism, Nationalism, and the Alienation
     of the Military   121

6   Mass Armies and the Professional Soldier   141

7   Middle-Class Society and the Rise of Military
     Professionalism: The Dutch Army 1589-1609   169

ABOUT THE AUTHOR   204

for Marian

PREFACE

The essays of Maury D. Feld collected in this volume are a valuable contribution to our understanding of military institutions. *The Structure of Violence: Armed Forces as Social Systems* is innovative with ideas yet rigorous in its attention to scholarly detail. Feld anticipated many of the new avenues which now guide students of military structures. Until quite recently, the main thrust of research was to view military institutions as self-contained organizational entities. Current endeavors, on the other hand, prefer to regard the military and civil spheres as interactive and partially coterminous. The sense of this broadened scope—always evident in Feld's writings—is captured in the contemporary preference for the term "armed forces and society," with its more inclusive connotations, as opposed to the more delimited term "military sociology."

Feld brings his talents of analysis to a variety of topics. We learn of the structured, and to some degree inevitable alienation, of the military professional from the body politic. Our understanding of authority in standard military forces is clarified by Feld's distinction between "leadership"—arising out of personal qualities in the field situation—and "command"—deriving from rational end-means calculations in the rear echelon. Professional military journals are subjected to content analysis informed by the sociology of knowledge. A typology of civil-military interface is presented which serves as a paradigm for predictions of self-conceptions of military elites. Prevailing modes of technology are insightfully reinterpreted as both causes and effects of transformations in military organization.

One of Feld's most significant contributions has been to dispel the view of a unilinear evolution of the modern military from the feudal order. He is especially revisionist in that the origins of military professionalism are placed much earlier than has been assumed in most extant military histories. Feld describes how the Dutch national army—a mercenary force without a social base in sixteenth-century Dutch society—achieved startling military effectiveness by substituting regular wages and discipline for heroic leadership and social solidarity.

Feld's social historical perspective highlights the nondeterministic development of military professionalism by emphasizing how variable sociopolitical structures interact with military institutions. But the leitmotiv in Feld's thought is much more controversial. This is the proposition that the standing army is as much the creator as the creature of the modern state. Until at least the advent of the industrial order, Feld argues, the post-feudal states of Europe were reflective and shaped by the values and social organization which first developed in the professional standing army.

The Structure of Violence is an exemplar of the way in which military history can be creatively blended with sociological constructs. These essays are indispensable to all those interested in the beginnings and subsequent elaborations of modern military institutions. The Inter-University Seminar on Armed Forces and Society is pleased to present this volume in its series of publications.

Charles C. Moskos, Jr.

ACKNOWLEDGEMENTS

The papers in this volume were written over two decades, 1956-1976. Apart from editorial corrections and attempts to clarify what seemed to be cloudy formulations, most of the essays are reprinted, more or less, in their original version. My recent article, "Middle Class Society and the Rise of Professionalism," is presented here in a much longer format than in the original journal publication. In addition, I have prepared a new paper entitled, "Discipline as a Social Force," which seeks to present my orientation to the analysis of military institutions. Taken as a whole, this collection of essays attempts to describe what I take to be the salient characteristics of the role allotted to military institutions in western societies: the establishment of particular norms of order and the inculcation of comprehensive value systems.

My debts are too many and varied to permit full listing. Two, however, deserve special acknowledgement. The late Edward L. Katzenbach, Jr. supported and encouraged my early work. Morris Janowitz, in our thirty years' friendship, has been a constant stimulus and scourge. He can be called into account for whatever merits this book may have. He pared its excesses and drove it toward relevance and intellectual commitment. I am not the only one who has learned from him that society—in and of itself—is "the moral equivalent of war."

The original essays appeared in the following: "A Typology of Military Organization," *Public Policy,* Volume VIII, Harvard University Press, 1958, pp. 3-40; "Information and Authority," *American Sociological Review,* Volume XXIV, No. 1, pp. 15-22; "Military Self-Image," *The New Military,* ed. by Morris Janowitz, Russell Sage Foundation, 1964, pp. 159-188; "Professionalism,

Nationalism," *Armed Forces and Society: Sociological Essays,* ed. by Jacques van Doorn, Mouton, 1968, pp. 55-70; "Mass Armies," Armed Forces and Society, Volume I, No. 2, 1975, pp. 191-224; "Middle Class Society," Armed Forces and Society, Volume I, No. 4, 1975, pp. 419-442. All are reprinted here by permission of the copyright holders. "Military Discipline as a Social Force" has never been printed before.

M. D. F.

1976

Chapter 1

MILITARY DISCIPLINE AS A SOCIAL FORCE

I

This collection of essays attempts to describe what I take to be the salient characteristics of the role allotted to military institutions in Western societies: the establishment of particular norms of order and the inculcation of comprehensive value systems. This is not to say that military institutions were created for that purpose or that they have explicitly been given that role. What we are dealing with is more in the way of a cultural and ideological accident. The central position traditionally given to military prowess as a masculine virtue in Western societies almost automatically presents the soldier as a natural leader. The destructive and coercive nature of his particular attributes makes him the one force society has to come to terms with, to harness or bribe into public service. Societies without armed forces may be possible. Political systems and soldiers are, however, in reality inseparable. The notion of the military vocation as a seminal political force is thus a theme deeply embedded in secular Western political thought. It lies at the heart of Plato's Republic. For Machiavelli it was the critical factor in the establishment of an autonomous community. In Max Weber we find it discussed as a germinal factor in the evolution of disciplined and rational political systems.[1]

Running counter to this is a theme evoked in both glorification and repugnance throughout the course of literature and the visual arts, the military profession as a destructive force. The poems of Homer and the monuments of the early empires are alike in their depiction of the warrior as a demonic agent.[2] This image persists throughout recorded history culminating in the work of the nineteenth-century artists Goya and Tolstoy, where the discipline of the armed forces and the bureaucratic rationality of their directing states stand in striking contrast to the brutality and destructiveness of their operations. In the twentieth century, the disparity has become too great to be intellectually encompassed.

Two examples illustrate this point. For Plato, the rationally organized society has its origin in the need to create a group of professional guardians (*Republic* 374B). Once this necessity has been acknowledged, it follows that these guardians must be trained so that they are hostile to outsiders and benign to fellow citizens. With this end in mind, Plato formulates his proposals for the education of elites, the distribution of property, and the division and role of social classes. His ideal state can be seen as a program for the creation of an effective and incorruptible armed force. The attainment of a rational and just social system not only depends upon such a body but also finds concrete realization in it.

By contrast, we have the testimony of Goya. In 1799, the last year of the century of Enlightenment, he published a volume of etchings, *The Caprichios.* The original frontispiece shows the artist asleep at his drawing board. Behind him rises a cloud of bats and owls, creatures of the night. This etching bears the legend, "The Sleep of Reason Brings forth Monsters."[3] As the subsequent etchings make clear, the mind freed from conventional controls allows life to assume its monstrous and perhaps basic forms. Reason's sleep is not a state of inactivity. It is rather a liberation of intellect from externally imposed notions of propriety.

Nine years later, French armies, the incarnation of reason armed, and rejecting social conventions, invaded Spain. The subsequent events directly stimulated another cycle of etchings, *The Disasters of War,* and two paintings, "The Second of May, 1808," and "The Third of May, 1808." The second can be treated as Goya's distillation of the experience of modern war. It depicts the nocturnal reprisal execution of a group of Spanish civilians. The victims, alive, dying, and dead, face a French firing squad. There is a striking contrast between the latern that illuminates the soldiers and the light of frenzy that shines from the faces of the victims. The soldiers stand in an almost somnambulistic rigidity, featureless, save for their projecting guns. They could be automatons. The civilians are sprawled and contorted in frantic postures. Even in death, their rage glares forth. "The sleep of reason" is embodied in an orderly controlled formation. The monsters it brings forth are the enraged civilians.[4]

For Goya, the rational structure of the military is a force that overwhelms civil conventions. In overwhelming them it releases those underlying horrors society has sought to conceal and tame. Society in its polite form is revealed to be no more than a Hobbesian state of nature. The drive to impose a general military order strips its rivals of any claim to dignity or sense. Just as in Plato's Republic, the nonmilitary elements have the alternative either of conforming to the standards of the guardians or of resorting to modes of behavior that deprive them of any claim to be treated as rational, responsible individuals.

This, of course, is social censorship in its broadest form. The rules of control are also the conditions of intelligibility. Reject them, and what you say or do makes no sense. Goya knew that there is a close relationship between censoring authority and the primitive forces of the unconscious, and that it is in dreams that their most direct confrontation takes place. In his eyes, the French armies were not primitive, uncontrolled masses but, rather, directly the reverse, a force released from conventions and formed and motivated entirely in terms of its own inner logic. If one accepted reason as the principle of order and discipline, the confrontation between French armies and Spanish civilians became a revelation of the latter's fundamental beastliness. The "sleep of reason" turns out to be more than a simple relaxation of control. It is a state whereby unconscious wishes are allowed full systematic play and can impose themselves on the disorganized fragments of everyday life. The sleep of reason permits the fantasy of all-regulating power to take coherent form.

Organized violence thus becomes the fulfillment of a dream, a dream wherein programmatic reason and naked power reinforce one another. Just as dreams struggle against the censorship of unconscious wish impulses,[5] the disciplined armed forces struggle against an ever present myth of everyday life; against society's unacceptable, if hardly unconscious, wish impulses for personal autonomy and society's belief, pitilessly described by Goya, that the pursuit of selfish pleasure will result in the union of innocence and bliss.

Disciplined armed forces—the term as here employed refers always to land armies—are the political program of the rational utopia, of the society which is both orderly and free; orderly because every member and every act is dedicated to the attainment of a common goal, free because every soldier either is a free contracted volunteer or has consciously accepted his role as part of the broader social contract to which he adheres. Disciplined military service invariably begins with explicit agreement and/or the taking of an oath.

Against this, we have the opposed utopian notion of natural man and his primitive golden age, with its belief that rational choice may not be the basis of personal happiness. But reason tells us that if we reject its guidance we have no one but ourselves to blame. The unnatural order imposed by reason, by external violence or by inner discipline is a punishment we deserve. It all comes from the fact that the way of reason is not a natural choice.

The contrast between these two contending utopian visions was clear to nineteenth-century liberal thinkers. The French philosopher Renan welcomed the German victory of 1870 as a justified demonstration of the superiority of organized Prussian intelligence over hedonistic French individuality.[6] As benevolent a thinker as William James called upon liberal society to organize its altruistic impulses under military forms and to find "a moral equivalent of war."[7] There is still talk today of "a war on poverty" and a "peace corps."

The emergence of armed forces into their modern professionalized, disciplined form has had the effect of transforming violence into a mode of order and making its victims appear to be destructive threats. The soldier is considered to be someone who has sacrificed his individuality in conquering impulses to which other men are all too prone. Captives of the romantic legend of heroic sacrifice, we welcome the notion that it is the function of discipline to maintain the social system rather than to increase firepower.

The evolution of the meaning of the word "discipline" is a record of this. According to the *Oxford English Dictionary*, it originally referred to the process of learning, and was the property of the disciple. As such it is the antithesis of doctrine, the state of achieved knowledge, that is, the property of the learned man, the doctor of philosophy. In current usage, discipline refers to an achieved condition rather than to a process. The progress of military professionalization was instrumental in this shift. It made amenability to instruction a state desirable in itself. By the mid-seventeenth century, we find the word "discipline" being used to denote a system and method for the maintenance of order. This sense of the word has steadily gained strength. In current discussions of educational theory, we frequently find the maintenance of classroom discipline treated as a problem distinct from and often at odds with the actual learning process.

The rise of professional armies played a major role in this shift. Toward the end of the sixteenth century, the Dutch developed a method whereby troops could be programmatically trained to combine maneuvering in an ordered fashion with the production of a steady and controlled rate of fire. This was perhaps the first major social activity organized by numbers. It was a model for the subsequent bureaucratic and industrial development of Europe.[8]

The implications of this were considerable. Ordinary individuals could be instructed in a systematic way to achieve, not the traditional goal of autonomous responsibility, i.e., to be learned men, but rather to become standardized and predictable members of a coordinated whole. Discipline came to connote not the individuals in the process of instruction but rather the perfected system to which such individuals were expected to conform. The critical word is "system." Only a systematic method of instruction can create a reliable system of control.

The demonstration of disciplined military efficiency transformed European notions about the relationship between man and authority. Machiavelli, who wrote before it had been truly achieved, saw, in the reestablishment of systematic, civic military training, a means of rekindling the antique Romans' virtue in their degenerate descendants. For him the state and its armed forces were still the sum of their individual members. For those who came afterward it had become something much greater. For Tolstoy, military discipline was a force that could momentarily raise a nondescript mediocrity like Captain Tushin to heroic heights.[9] Max Weber believed that a political version of military discipline could make ordinary citizens members of heroic society.[10]

It is not that discipline sanitized warfare. The idealization of military virtues has very little to do with observable facts. Plato, Machiavelli, and Weber had, as much as Goya and Tolstoy, concrete experience of the destructive and subversive effects of political wars and heroic commanders. The fact that they saw in military systems the elements of a rational order must be taken with the terrible seriousness it deserves. For them, the martial outlook was the unique sources of certain essential social values. The maintenance of armed forces and the training of their leaders involved far more than the creation of a means of defense and an instrument of policy. It was the matrix for the labeling and diffusion of the basic values on which the very cohesion of society depended.

In its most naked sense, the simple existence of an armed force answers the question of how much an individual is worth to society and how much society is worth to him. The decisions—about who is to serve, in what capacity, and for what sort of compensation—describe the social policies of a political system, often long before it is itself aware of the need for or the existence of such a concept. Military service is one area of social activity that continually calls into question the costs of commonly shared goals and that deliberately sets a price on human life. As the feudal elements of holy service and of hereditary station and duty receded, the armed forces became notable as an arena where enlisted men risked everything for a pittance and where the leaders strove for inestimable wealth and glory. Each in his manner "saved the sum of things for pay." It is no accident that the military structure of authority is directly translatable into that fundamental symbolic order, the price system, and that it was, in all probability, the pioneer in the graduated wage scale.[11] It is also no accident that professional, disciplined armies emerged as part of the process of European secularization.

II

The late sixteenth-century military inventions of disciplined firepower and professionalized leadership thus had a profound effect on the evolution of modern Western society. The sixteenth century saw the earliest application of two of modern Western society's basic concepts: marginal economic man, and rationally trained and rationally oriented leadership. The enlisted ranks of the new style armies constituted the lowest level at which human beings could be employed at a living wage. Military service was the social skill that could be acquired by virtually any adult male. Discipline was the way of life for those who had demonstrated their incapacity to learn anything else. From the mid-seventeenth century until The French Revolution, the military rank and file were the riffraff and scourings of society, those with no evident skill or resources other than the unimpaired use of their physical faculties, and at times not even quite that. Immediately before the emergence of the new discipline, battlefields had been dominated by the presence of certain elite popular groups—English longbowmen, Swiss pikemen, Spanish men-at-arms. All these had been the possessors of certain traditional skills, developed in the context of their particular communities, and never really transplantable to other contexts. Each represented a unique military resource of its society.

The gun was a great leveler. It can be said to have created the concept of marginal economic man. Within the context of the new discipline, it not only made every soldier an equal threat, it also represented a technique that almost anyone could be taught, whose teaching could be achieved within a relatively short period, and whose application required no more than executing the instructions of the supervisor. The disciplined armed force was the proto-factory system. Like the factory system in the early industrial age, it demanded an abandonment of all traditional notions of behavior and the acceptance of the new system as an all-encompassing environment.

Similarly, the emergent professional officer corps was the earliest member of the now familiar complex of administrative agencies and educational institutions whereby the state manufactures the matrix of skills and attitudes it considers necessary for its continuation of growth. The new officer corps fostered a chain of ranks and assignments, with explicit if not always observed criteria of aptitudes and experience for each. By the eighteenth century, admission to the officer corps of almost every European army was governed by certain standards of education, and by the assumption that professional advancement entailed a process of professional growth. The proletarianization of the enlisted man placed an increasing premium on the organizational and managerial skills of the officer and implanted the germ of a meritocratic notion within the ranks.

It is ironic that the administrative problems of professional standing armies should have stimulated the emergence of the earliest European bureaucratic civil service.[12] The new armies provided a model for the bureaucratic states. They inverted the feudal order where social position determined rank, where kings commanded armies, dukes subdivisions, etc., to one where rank determined social position. Army commanders became dukes, divisional commanders barons, etc. The state as an organized entity was conceived as a war-making apparatus, a system for financing wars and distributing the profits thereof. It established itself along the lines of a two-tiered structure: a system of offices, rewards, and honors for those who directly served its purposes;

and a system of fiscal and physical exactions for those who did not. Service in the ranks was the lot of those who otherwise served no useful purpose, who could not contribute in either income or labor to the maintenance of the administrative apparatus and its members. The discipline of controlled firepower thus played the role of being the basic form of productive activity for those whom neither crafts, agriculture, nor commerce could absorb.

The rise of nationalism added yet another variable to this process. The patriotic motivation which came from the conscious membership in a nation-state was harnessed to the creation of armies of a hitherto unprecedented size and of a firepower capacity which took into account the technological resources of the Industrial Revolution.[13] Nationalism gave the state an ideological as well as an administrative dimension. Enlisted men were enrolled, not only on the negative basis of their marginal social and economic utility, but also on the positive ground of their membership in a territorial and linguistic community. National military service became the basic unit of social affiliation, the act that absorbed the individual into the service of the state and that entitled him to the fundamental benefits it conferred, i.e., the vote and eligibility for higher civil positions.

This shift in the basis of enlisted recruitment from the negative grounds of social and economic alienation to the positive ones of political and ideological commitment transformed the nature and role of disciplinary and tactical structure. Neither the time, the money, nor the personnel was available to drill the rapidly mobilized mass armies into the mechanical proficiency of numerically controlled firepower. Moreover, the positively motivated new style of soldier did not require the system of absolute control of his negatively regarded predecessor. The old order of tactics and discipline had been in part inspired by the well-founded fear that any relaxation of discipline and control would result in mass desertion and panic. The eighteenth-century professional soldier regarded his rational all-encompassing system as the only possible antidote to the spiritless individuality of nonaristocratic orders. Constraint and habit alone could make the lower orders serviceable to the state. The notion of an ideological, an inner-directed, patriotism was inconceivable to them.

The popular levies of the French Revolution demonstrated that there were other political and military possibilities. Extended franchise and the new notion of the state as a system of offices and responsibilities open to all its inhabitants made every citizen potentially a positively motivated instrument of policy. Using tactics as much forced on them by the necessity of rapidly raising large armies with a diminished and unreliable professional cadre as by the desire to take advantage of the unique ideological fervor of their enlisted material, the French developed a set of tactics based on open formations and the unregulated use of firearms. Military discipline, however, did not disappear with these innovations. But it was transformed, being internalized within the enlisted structure and no longer a total product of the skills and controls of professional officers. The era of mass popular armies was one in which the primary group replaced the alienated conglomerate.[14]

Technologically speaking, this development was stimulated by the development of rapid-fire hand weapons. The armies of the French Revolution were, in their way, an aberration—armies effectively motivated by ideological fervor. The Napoleonic armies reverted to mass tactics and professional controls. Nonetheless, the precedent of popular levies had been set, and the social structure of armies responded accordingly. Unexpectedly, the French noncommissioned officers of that period played a responsible and heroic role in the conduct of operations. This certainly was a novel development, if written records are any proof. Partly it was due to the fact that the popular ideology of the period made them more authentic leaders than the privileged members of the officer caste. Napoleon, after all, fostered a cult around himself, using the image of the "little corporal." It was also due to the fact that the abandonment of tight formations made the established system of discipline obsolete. It is worth noting that in the first half of the nineteenth century the officer corps of the Prussian army by and large opposed the adoption of the breech-loading rifle, on the grounds that its simplicity and efficiency would encourage individual initiative and thereby weaken their control of the lower ranks. As a matter of fact, when adopted it almost immediately resulted in a rise in both the numbers and the prestige of noncoms. Noncoms quickly emerged as a privileged caste whose authority rested on their ability to maintain internal cohesion where formerly there had been an almost total dependence on external control.[15]

The new style of noncommissioned officer was in effect made a member of the bureaucratic structure, with the privileges and personal security accompanying such status. More significant, noncommissioned status became an avenue of social mobility, opening higher ranks and higher society to its members and their descendants. In the caste-ridden German armies of World War I, Ludendorff and Groener, the two major Western Front commanders at the war's end, were the sons of senior noncommissioned officers.

The social effect of military professionalism thus stemmed from the two concepts for which it was the innovating European agency: bureaucratic politicization and marginal social utility. The army became the instrument whereby the state established its minimum standard of civic value and its graduated scale of social rewards. The discipline of the armed forces came to represent the most primitive form of active political life. State activity itself was structured in terms of a hierarchy of responsibility for enforcement. The professional officer corps served as a model for the process whereby the state sought to create, instruct, and motivate the instruments of its policies—or, more precisely, of the form of social order it sought to embody. Starting with the Prussian garrison state, a system of administration emerged in which the skills of the functionaries defined the duties of the subjects.

The initiator of this system was Frederick William of Brandenburg, the Great Elector, characterized recently as "this *Dutch-trained* impetuous climber . . . a highly talented and imaginative innovator who developed into an importer of novel instruments of domination and a daring improvisor of institutional reforms."[16] His basic technique was quite simple. He deprived local agencies of their traditional autonomy and made the procedures of day-to-day urban and rural existence subject to the dictates of a body of officials trained according to his standards and responsible only to him.[17]

In similar vein, the armies of Western Europe were restructured about the creation of a fighting force whose skills were to be measured solely in terms of their responsiveness to their officers' commands. The first reform was based on the creation of a body of experts who were the exclusive possessors of key administrative techniques. The second reform was based on the creation of an administrative area where the subject population possessed no inherent technical qualifications whatsoever. The durability and superiority of this complex model was demonstrated by the fact that, though the mass army was the invention of revolutionary France, its perfection as a military device took place in conservative Prussia.

The doctrine of the rights of man did, nonetheless, present a challenge to this system, a challenge which was ingeniously met. Mercenary armies were replaced by citizens' armies. The qualifying trait of responsiveness to the officer's commands was replaced by one of responsiveness to the call of civic duty. The army and the state became in essence inseparable. Obedience was the basic attribute of the subject population. This solution simultaneously increased both the motivation and the supply of enlisted members. It was, however, a solution that posed special problems of its own making.

The old order was based on the juncture of two groups each in its own way estranged from economically productive society. The officer corps were a body preponderantly drawn from the rural aristocracy and dominated by its ethos. This group professed a revulsion for productive or moneymaking activity. Their income was assumed to be based entirely on their service to the state. Dependence on other sources of wealth, either directly or through inheritance, was a stigmatizing factor.

On the other hand, there were the enlisted ranks, a collection of able-bodied men, incapable, for whatever reason, of adjusting themselves to the processes and patterns of ordinary society— marginal individuals who also chose to gain their livelihood through absolute submission to the dictates of the state. The officer's role was, however, assumed to be based on merit; the enlisted man's, on fate. The enlisted man, moreover, was below society, not above it. As such, he was not included in the administrative apparatus of the state.

The adoption of national service changed this. Now the solid citizens joined the armies and the marginal ones were rejected. Illiteracy, for example, formerly a dominant characteristic of enlisted ranks, became a disqualifying trait. Social productivity, rather than being a drawback, became the dominant criterion of military value. This was a revolution from below which radically affected the nature and composition of the officer corps. Henceforth, in steadily increasing measure, the skills and professional criteria of the higher ranks reflected the skills and professional criteria of civilian society.[18]

The effect this had on the discipline and composition of the enlisted ranks was perhaps of even greater importance. With military service transformed into an index of political affiliation, the officer corps were no longer able to treat the lower ranks as a blank page upon which they were free to print whatever set of instructions they wished. If discipline meant the acceptance of a condition of economic marginality, politicization meant participation in the system by state-generated rewards. Discipline and training had henceforth to take into account not only reward but also the assumed national character. Both were now to be judged in terms of the benefits they conferred upon their subjects.

The initial reaction was, as already stated, the adoption of the concept of military life as a "carrière ouverte aux talents." Noncommissioned grades were recognized as positions of responsibility and privilege, and even as legitimate avenues to official status. At the same time, the military establishment in general and the officer corps in particular were charged with a positive responsibility toward civilian recruits. Transforming them into effective soldiers was no longer considered sufficient. Military service, it was now asserted, would change its human material into better citizens and more valuable members of society.

This positive orientation made military service more popular and more controversial. In effect, it gave enlisted men rights, particularly the right to be improved by their experience. The military establishment expanded its role to make place for the claim that those entering its service would, among other things, not only be physically and morally improved but would also reemerge into the outside world with acquired skills that would entitle them to more rewarding civilian careers.

III

Increased manpower requirements and advancing military technology have thus inverted the concept of military discipline. In its original form, military discipline was regarded as a device for the creation of groups formed according to the state's own image of rational public service, a device which accordingly operated on material presumably free of any internalized guiding principles. Early military formations therefore operated in opposition to and even in repression of autonomous social forces. They were equally the scourge of the peasant and the tormentor of the bourgeoisie. We have only to look at Great Britain, where opposition to standing armies was traditionally associated with the defense of local and individual liberties.

The advent of national service and the constantly growing need for rank-and-file soldiers endowed with nonmarginal skills transformed this pattern. Since military discipline now had to deal with enlisted masses whose basic social utility was already confirmed by membership in the national community, and to attract specialists whose skills were already rewarded in the marketplace, the concept and effectiveness of military discipline were subjected to novel pressures. By almost imperceptible stages, discipline evolved from being an instrument of the extension of the authority of the state into being a process whereby the state's notion of its social responsibilities was constantly being broadened. The concepts of politicization and marginal social utility were redefined. Originally they were delimiting devices, employed to divide those who had social status or political privilege from those who did not. In their present usage, they are leveling devices designed to eliminate distinctions within the armed forces.

This fact is cogently illustrated by schemes of military reform now being actively pursued. These can be described as proceeding along the lines of two conceptual models. One seeks to maximize politicization and to eliminate the marginal components of military service. The other stresses the enrichment of marginal social value and the elimination of the political claims of military authority. Examples of these impulses at work are to be found in the contemporary American and Israeli armies.

The programs now under way for the creation of an all-volunteer U.S. Army provide us with an example of an armed force where military service at every level is to be treated as a form of public office. The all-volunteer force is a patent attempt to escape from a previous system where enlisted service was regarded as a social sacrifice imposed on the less fortunate members of society. In the reformed army, every soldier will be treated as a career specialist, a member of a craft or skill group. This stands in ironic contrast to the origins of discipline, where enlisted men qualified precisely in terms of not being so. Inherent in this program is the notion of the enlisted ranks as the training groups for the lower civil service. While in the army, the volunteer enlisted man will be in the first stage of a career that can be extended after early retirement with transfer of rank, pension privileges, etc., into other branches of government.[19]

The disciplinary implications of such a force are far-reaching. There will be obviously a minimum of external controls, of authoritative devices based on the superior skill and knowledge of the officer corps. Motivation and performance criteria will be assumed to come largely from the enlisted man's own craft ethic and from his awareness of the material rewards of prolonged and efficient service. This long march brings us back to the English longbowman and the Swiss pikeman of the late Middle Ages.

Ever since its inception, the Israeli army has pursued the disciplinary model of an armed force designed to raise the marginal social value of the citizens of that country. Its training programs were designed not only to eliminate social differences among the subjects of national services but also to minimize protocol distinctions based on rank. The concept of enlisted indoctrination pursued by the Israeli army envisaged a process whereby marginal social groups would be raised through military service to a higher level of social and economic participation. The policy pursued toward officers was one which envisaged a rapid turnover and return to civilian life and an officer corps that had a minimal claim to a corporate existence of its own. The discipline of such a body would be externally imposed. The officer corps by its demonstrated willingness for personal sacrifice would impose its standards of behavior on the enlisted ranks.

There are paradoxical elements in the expectations and results of these two models. The politicization of the American army, i.e., the universal transformation of the military role into a form of public office, is expected to have among its results a marked decrease in the political role and influence of the army officer. His status will become that of a strictly subordinated civil servant. To the degree that his responsibility for disciplining enlisted men becomes less direct, his popular constituency and public responsibility will be diminished. In Israel, on the other hand, the depoliticization of officer rank has created a tendency for a military meritocracy to emerge that has a strong social and political corporate influence. The officer is able to present himself, not as a member of a privileged group, but as the successful leader of a popular force bound by a common experience of public service.

The U.S. Army's rejection of the notion of marginal social value is based on a role concept that envisages its future use largely as an instrument of deterrence rather than as an active operational force. Soldiers' lives at every level have become too valuable to be risked. Military ventures have been relegated to the realm of the accidental. In adopting the concept of marginal social utility, on the other hand, the Israeli forces have accepted as explicit the assumption that costly military operations will be a regular part of their pattern of existence. The soldier's sense of his social value will be elevated to justify the sacrifices expected of him. The higher the value, it is assumed, the greater the risk. This is also a peculiar inversion of the original notion.

What has disappeared in both cases is the idea of civil society as an adversary force. Within the nation-state, the soldier no longer considers himself to be threatened by unorganized social forces.

His rivals, if any, are competing bureaucratic systems, agencies that propose alternative public careers. The rationalizing concepts of which he was once the revolutionary proponent have become the furniture of everyday life.

NOTES

1. The pertinent passages in Plato are to be found in the *Republic,* especially Book II; in Machiavelli, throughout the *Discourses on Livy* and the *Art of War;* in Max Weber, in *Wirtschaft und Gesellschaft,* pt. 3, chap. 5, pp. 642-649. I know of no extended discussion of this aspect of Plato and Weber; for Machiavelli there is Isaiah Berlin's excellent essay, "The Originality of Machiavelli," in Myron P. Gilmore, ed., *Studies on Machiavelli* (G. C. Sansono, 1972), pp. 147-206.
2. Rachael Bespaloff, *On the Iliad* (New York: Harper Torchbooks, 1972).
3. This was for its age a familiar theme. See Hobbes, *Leviathan,* pt. 1, chap. 2. "The most difficult discerning of a man's dream, from his waking thoughts, is then, when by some accident we observe not that we have slept; which is easy to happen to a man full of fearful thoughts, and whose conscience is much troubled; and that sleepeth, without the circumstances of going to bed or putting off his clothes, as one that noddeth in a chair." Schopenhauer, *The World as Will and Idea,* bk. 1, 8; "I cannot refrain from adding that, so long as truth is absent, error will have free play, as owls and bats in the night"; also Hegel, "the owl of Athena takes flight at dusk."
4. Examples of this contrast of frenzied civilians and controlled soldiers are found throughout *The Disasters of War;* e.g., No. 36, "Populacho," murderous civilians, No. 40, "With Reason or Without It," military executioners.
5. Sigmund Freud, *A General Introduction to Psychoanalysis* (Garden City, N.Y.: Doubleday, 1938), p. 133.
6. Edmond and Jules de Goncourt, *Journal* (Monaco: 1956), 9:32.
7. William James, "The Moral Equivalent of War," in *Essays on Faith and Morals* (London: Longmans, Green, 1947), pp. 311-328.
8. See chapter 7 of this book.
9. Leo Tolstoy, *War and Peace,* bk. 2, chaps. 13, 15, 16. It is worth noting that Tolstoy abandoned this notion of war for a political philosophy of pacifism and anarchism.
10. Marianne Weber, *Max Weber, Ein Lebensbild* (Tubingen: 1926), pp. 664-665.
11. Fritz Redlich, "The German Military Enterpriser and His Work," Vol. I, *Vierteljahrschrift für Social und Wirtschaftsgeschichte,* Beiheft 47 (Wiesbaden, *Franz Steiner Verlag GMBH),* p. 458.
12. Otto Hintze, "The Commissary and His Significance," in *The Historical Essays of Otto Hintze,* ed. Felix Gilbert (London: Oxford University Press, 1975), pp. 267-301.
13. See chapter 6 of this book.
14. See Morris Janowitz and Edward A. Shils, "Cohesion and Disintegration in the Wehrmacht in World War II," in Morris Janowitz, *Military Conflict* (Beverly Hills, Calif.: Sage, 1976), pp. 177-220.
15. Dennis Showalter, *Railroads and Rifles: Soldiers, Technology and the Unification of Germany* (Archon Books, 1975), pp. 91-104.

16. Hans Rosenberg, *Bureaucracy, Aristocracy and Autocracy: The Prussian Experience 1660-1815* (Boston: Beacon, 1966), p. 34 (my italics).
17. F. L. Carsten, *The Origins of Prussia* (London: Oxford University Press, 1954), p. 279 ff.
18. See chapter two of this book.
19. M. Janowitz, "U.S. Forces and the Zero Draft," Janowitz, *Military Conflict*, pp. 239-283; see also Major James S. Dickey, "Politicization of the Military: A Personal Statement," in *Military Force and American Society,* ed. Bruce M. Russett and Alfred Stepan (New York: Harper & Row, 1973), pp. 17-33.

Chapter 2

A TYPOLOGY OF MILITARY ORGANIZATION

Introduction

War has usually been represented as an instrument of policy and of romance. Participants and observers, with only an occasional exception, have found something in it transcending ordinary affairs and pointing to some broader and more coherent scheme of ends and aspirations. Considering the expanse of history taken up by military enterprises, this approach can perhaps be credited to a prudent desire on man's part to preserve his image of human dignity from a destructive interpretation. At any rate, the soldier has conventionally been presented as the servant of some aspect of the ideal. The conditions of his service, monstrous as they may have appeared, have rarely been described as commonplace.

This idealization has furthered the process of the isolation of the soldier as a distinct social type. Men who have mastered the tools of violence have stood apart from those who have not done so. Dedication to the techniques of war has created patterns of behavior and outlook sufficiently coherent and explicit to bind the practitioners of these techniques into a distinct and exclusive social entity.

These patterns, representing principles of military organization both as practiced and as idealized by its participating members, are

Reprinted from Public Policy, *Volume VII, 1958, pp. 3-40.*

the subject of this chapter. The word "military" refers both to the apparatus of leadership set up within the military and to the arrangements made by the latter to ensure its material support. Variations in the intensity and scope of such groups and of their activities are, of course, possible, and official recognition does not always imply social acceptance. But social acceptance is essential. Regular armies wither if they lack public support, while irregular groups prosper through its possession. Reduce their numbers and effectiveness below a nebulous minimum and they are no longer soldiers but bandits. Success and expansion, on the other hand, have transformed disturbers of the peace into sovereign entities.

The commitment to and the support of a specific social-political system is inherent in the nature of military organization. Since the application of violence is its primary occupation, the existence of a military organization presupposes enemies beyond the bounds of the institutions from which it draws support. In order to function as self-perpetuating entities, armies require external objectives. The martial spirit turned inward is self-destructive, an instrument for razing the platform on which it stands.

The absence of the stimulus of external enemies can, as in feudal systems, atomize a society dominated by the military into a complex of violently competing communities.[1] Normally, however, the presence of hostile neighbors place the soldier in the ranks of the established order. Whatever the forms of his service may be, the political and social system out of which he operates gives the soldier scope and direction. Internal disturbances are clearly subversive. They corrode the tools of his trade and distract him from his major responsibility, that of the defense and extension of frontiers. In a way which is both logical and unique, armies are a dedicated instrument of political institutions.

All known political systems have boundaries, limits to the effectiveness of their means of nonviolent persuasion. They all, therefore, recognize occasions that sanction the use of force. Every state has its own army, designed for what it considers to be its preservation. Differences in the missions for which armies are organized provide an essential criterion in the analysis and description of political types as well as of military systems. In the kindred fields of politics and war, the army and the state interact and influence one another. Politicians believe that their concepts of civic virtues and aptitudes should find expression in the armies they legislate into existence. Soldiers look for political institutions which conform to their standards of military efficiency.

In this debate, the ill-defined structure of civil institutions, which avoid a rigid identification between the interests of the individual and those of the group, is opposed to the parochial self-consciousness of military organizations. The variety of civil institutions is balanced by the solidarity of the military ones. As a social entity, an armed force enjoys an exceptional degree of cohesion and of ideological consciousness.[2] It conceives of its activities in terms of corporate well-being, while the majority of other social formations conceive of theirs in terms of individual failure and success. The military in its role as political and social guardian stands on the frontier not of felicity but of crisis. Particular aptitudes and strivings for self-expression must be suppressed. The personality of the officer is determined by the responsibilities and the objectives of his organization.[3]

In discussing the nature of military types, then, we must define the role and the position specific armies claim in the social structure and the form of the beliefs in which such claims find expression. The hypothesis to be developed here is that such claims and beliefs constitute the various forms of what is commonly referred to as the "military mind"—that the emotional and intellectual positions under consideration are the models guiding the modes of organization and employment of military forces, and that this complex of "ideal types" provides the critical apparatus according to which military men submit experience to judgment. In justification of this approach, I can do no better than cite the argument of Professor J. L. Talmon:

What this study is concerned with is a state of mind, a way of feeling, a disposition, a pattern of mental, emotional and behavioristic elements, best compared to the set of attitudes engendered by a religion. Whatever may be said about the significance of the economic or other factors in the shaping of beliefs, it can hardly be denied that the all-embracing attitudes of this kind, once crystallized, are the real substance of history. The concrete elements of history, the acts of politicians, the aspirations of people, the ideas, values, preferences and prejudices of an age, are the outward manifestations of its religion in the widest sense.[4]

THE STRUCTURAL ENVIRONMENT

Ideological distinctions among military types are based on the manner in which organized violence can play a role in a given society. According to the simplest political classification of wars, armies may be called upon to attack or to defend. Their leaders, by equally simple social criteria, may come from within the society or be drawn from outside of it. In their origins, moreover, they may either be members of an exclusive caste or be broadly selected. In any case, they represent a highly specialized group, dedicated to acts which fall beyond the normal processes of government, and as such imply a definition of war as an event which, socially and politically, is extraordinary. There is, in addition, the archetypal case where the army, the society, and the state are regarded as one and the same entity, where war is regarded as the normal condition, where the structure of society is the order of battle, where discipline is law, and where status is equivalent to military rank.

According to these categories, five structural types can be formulated: military elites[5] that maintain themselves as an alien body superimposed on a conquered society; military elites that maintain themselves as an alien body distributed within a conquered society; military elites which make their place in society as members of a native and politically oriented aristocracy; military elites which qualify themselves in terms of some socially oriented scale of aptitudes; and, finally, military elites whose composition corresponds to the overall structure of power within a nation in arms.

These types and their corresponding political situations can be categorized as follows:

A. External dominance — Imperial
B. Internal dominance — Feudal
C. Closed equality — National
D. Open equality — Representative
E. Ideological equality — Totalitarian

Table 6: Typology of Armies in Terms of Relationship to Total Society

Structure	Policy Base	Self Image	Policy Role	Social Model	Control	Indoctrination
A External Dominance	Imperial	Civilization	Aggrandize	Three Class	Flow of Officers	Officer-Enlisted Man Emulation
B Internal Dominance	Feudal	Blood Elite	Legitimize	Two Class	Flow of Status	Officer-Officer Emulation
C Closed Equality	National	Heart and Brain	Formalize	Organic Classless	Flow of Conscripts	Unit - Unit Emulation
D Open Equality	Representative	Experts	Embody	Entrepreneurial Classless	Flow of Technological Instruments	Branch-Branch Emulation
E Ideological Equality	Totalitarian	Charisma	Propagate	Communal	Flow of Ideologically Meaningful Missions	Army - Army Emulation

External Dominance

The first type, that of *external* dominance, describes society as organized by violence and conquest. This type represents the extreme in separation between a military organization and its supporting society. Under external dominance the elite are not only ipso facto soldiers but also wholly absorbed within the structure of the military organization. All that lies outside that organization is explicitly servile and inferior.

In its political form, that of empire, external dominance has represented a vocational ideal. Careers in its service have offered an alternative to the humdrum routine, the "political" contaminations, and the nonmilitary atmosphere which make military life at home "impure" and unpalatable. In one of its most publicized modern examples, the French Foreign Legion, it has assumed a mythical status of adventurous "escape."

Whatever the attractions of escape may be, however, they are too negative and too individual to serve in the indoctrination of a corporate and disciplined body. The self-image appropriate to the imperial soldier is not that of a man who is fleeing his society but of one dedicated to its institutions and its virtues, those of civilization. The lands and persons of outsiders, Aztecs, Incas, Gauls, North Africans, or Hindus, are regarded as his legitimate material and prey. The inability of the conquered peoples and societies to resist demonstrates their state of nature[6] and proves that their condition is antithetical to sovereign responsibility. They are, therefore, ideologically no more than part of the material resources for some more complexly organized society— for a real civilization.

In military terms, the self-image of civilization is transformed into the policy role of aggrandizement. While the conquests of an external dominant army may eventually result in an increase in the commerce and security of its parent state, the mission which colors the actions of such a force is that of spreading civilization over a wider area. Economic exploitation is the function and the reward of groups other than the military.

An external dominant organization cannot come to a position of rest. It is obliged to prove continually that civilization is the monopoly of its leaders. The continuance in power of any other group is, therefore, an affront to reason. Their existence in a nonconquered state represents a menace to civilization, since it is a concrete manifestation of a denial of the incapacity of natives to govern themselves. Native institutions can, then, have no legitimacy other than that which the convenience and the tolerance of the conquerors bestow upon them. An external dominant army once embarked on its career of aggrandizement is obliged to continue until nature and desolation provide it with limits.[7]

The details of government do not, however, fall within the province of the imperial military elite. Members of this group, while they may consider themselves equal to the task of formulating the broad outlines of social policy, are not numerous enough to immerse themselves in the particulars of its execution. The nearly total absorption in and dedication to military life which an external dominant organization demands of its leaders render an autonomous administrative apparatus necessary.[8]

An external dominant organization must, therefore, create an auxiliary class, a stratum of administrators and middlemen between itself and the conquered. These may be lower-caste members of the military organization's home society, local collaborators, or migrant adventurers; the sole requirement is nonmembership in the military elite. The three classes thus created represent three worlds, authority at the top, privilege in the middle, and subservience below.

As a social model, this tripartite arrangement serves many functions. It emphasizes the distinction between rulers and ruled. It maintains a strict specialization for the military calling and prevents the emergence of nonorganizational interests among the elite and their soldiers. It permits efficient exploitation of the conquered area. It erects a buffer class whose members can be sacrificed to the complaints of the exploited without too great damage to the morale of the ruling body. It creates a responsible administrative body for nonmilitary functions. It keeps the military free for further ventures.

This model cannot, however, provide total support for an imperial army. Such an army, no matter how striking its success, can never be self-sustaining. One factor binds the imperial army to the metropolitan society and keeps it responsive to that society's dictates and controls: an imperial state cannot recruit its leadership cadres from the conquered peoples. In an order established by conquest, the admission of the conquered to positions of military leadership represents a retreat. If the conquered are capable of military responsibility, they are capable of managing the rest of their affairs.

The resulting necessity of recruiting leaders from areas in which it is by definition forbidden to operate, and over which it has no direct control, presents an external dominant army with its particular problem of indoctrination. The objectives here are twofold. Officer recruits must come to identify themselves with the external dominant army as an entity which, while serving in distant areas, incarnates the metropolitan homeland. Officer recruits must likewise place themselves at the head of and gain a sense of kinship and common interest with the body of their alien command.

This second objective is the critical one. Imperial service tends simultaneously both to exaggerate and to bridge the distance between leadership cadres and the ranks. On the one hand, the mystique of command is intensified. Officers regard themselves as agents of a spiritual force, civilization, and view their service as a mission as well as a profession.[9] On the other hand, the pressures of garrison life tighten the bonds between all ranks. The essential division is between conquered and conquerors, not between leaders and led. The belief that all the forms of nonmilitary life are hostile to them gives external dominant soldiers a community of interest.

The conflict of these two objectives inclines an external dominant army to prefer aliens to nationals as enlisted men. The factor of common nationality can, in an external dominance situation, undermine discipline. If the ideological justification of authority is the possession of a superior standard of civilization, the enlisted men from the metropolitan base share that quality with officers. At least, they may believe that they should share it, and the burden of subordination will be increased by the loneliness and monotony of garrison life.

Moreover, the presence of fellow citizens in the ranks of external dominant armies decreases the range of their autonomy. When the soldiers involved have families with votes, or at least with voices, the metropolitan base is likely to maintain a greater interest in their operations and hold them in greater responsibility for casualties incurred. This may tend to inhibit an army's range of action and to increase the intensity of its externally imposed controls.

With "native" soldiers, on the other hand, all these problems disappear. Such soldiers, drawn either from areas outside the field of conquest or from select groups within it, strengthen their commander's hand. Because they are consciously chosen and distinguished from the mass of the uncivilized, it is assumed that they will recognize themselves as being in their commander's debt. They can be expected to find honor and achievement rather than imposition in their subjection to civilized command.

The use of select natives as soldiers has resulted in a particularly romantic concept of imperial leadership. The radical opposition of external dominant service to all nonmilitary forms of life prevents its leaders from employing arguments of social or political utility in defense of its organizational characteristics. It is necessary that imperial armies be presented as the spontaneous product of civilized values rather than as the instrument of devious political calculations.[10] Its traits must be explained on a purely military basis. Service must be presented as an act of self-realization rather than as one of social purpose; the military life must be described as the morality of those who are expressly created for it and, therefore, would otherwise be lost among civilian ways.[11] The native is, therefore, declared to be chosen on the basis of his natural military qualities. The mantle of the noble savage is decked about his person, justifying his selection. In this he is opposed to the other natives, ignoble savages, who are not worthy to serve in the imperial ranks. That the noble savage generally turns out to be rather more primitive than the ignoble one serves to prove that no civilization at all is preferable to a false one, and emphasizes that true culture which qualifies his leaders for their particular role.

In this glorified form, the native recruit becomes an instrument in overcoming an essential ambiguity in the imperial ideology. The quality of civilization which, enshrined in the metropolitan homeland, is regarded as the justification of conquest is, when confronted by martial necessity, judged to be antithetical to the military virtues. Its attributes of moral and intellectual self-sufficiency run counter to the requirements of discipline. Civilization as a personal quality is, therefore, insufficient to transform a metropolitan recruit into a military leader. It must be remodeled into a collective attribute, one which comes not from national origin but from organizational role. For this transformation, contact with the soldiers is necessary. Though he is not civilized, the noble

savage is assumed to possess an equally valid quality, the martial
proficiency which makes him eligible for service. Carried one step
further, the native trooper—Ghurka or Houmi—becomes the
personification of Mars, and thus an instrument in the indoctrination of officer candidates whose civilization is beyond the
questioning of the rank and file but whose military proficiency is
subject to their doubt.

In order to display his capacity for military leadership, the
officer candidate enters into competition with and proves himself
the martial peer of the men under him; an effort which in practice
involves his stripping himself of all his original attributes save that
of rank. His own leadership claims are thus safeguarded in this
emulatory process—provided that he does not fail to prove himself
a "soldier." Since he is meeting the native on the latter's terms,
the quality of "civilization" is not contested and remains his badge
of leadership. The right to exercise such leadership, however,
becomes the gift of the military organization, conferred on the
basis of its own criteria and not those of the metropolitan homeland.
The tested recruit, after stripping himself bare, regains his
birthright by proving himself capable of taking on the responsibility of his organization role.[12]

Internal Dominance

Military forces of internal dominance structure characterize a
society in the process of being settled by its conquerors. The
condition of conquest is here transformed into a social norm, that
of feudalism.[13] Unlike the imperial army, which leaves the
conquered society fundamentally unchanged and is content with a
situation guaranteeing it an undisputed monopoly of power and an
undisturbed collection of tribute, feudal institutions seek to
transform native institutions into a social expression of the power
and the possessions of individual members of its military elite.

For the career soldier, then, an internal dominance organization
represents a condition where martial proficiency is translated into
a clear and concrete stake in the social order. Value as a soldier

corresponds to landed wealth, proficiency as a leader to the effectiveness of political authority. War is regarded as the natural condition of man, and society is based on the factors governing it.

Social organization and militant man are thus united. But individual valor is a sufficient basis neither for the erection of an efficient military system nor for a stable social order. Its possessors are all too subject to fate and misfortune.[14] More important, it is not sufficient to guarantee the secure possession of the status and the property which individual soldiers have been able to obtain. While the "companion of the conqueror" may be able, through force and cunning, to maintain himself in power, what assurance is there that his natural heirs will be endowed with similar gifts in similar degree? Establishing a society on the pure pattern of individual attributes invites a revolution and a redistribution of power with every campaign or generation.

Since candidates for a feudal elite are not in general doctrinaire revolutionaries, some bond of common interest must be created— in this case, the self-image of membership in a blood-elite. Social preeminence becomes the expression of virtues handed down from father to son. Members of an internal dominant elite claim that a given social political system is sanctified because they personally are directing it. With sometimes authentic and more often falsified pedigrees, they declare themselves to be the legitimate heirs of those who have always ruled.[15]

To counter the claims of individual aggressiveness, the collective understanding is created that the existing division of property corresponds to the requirements of a minimum degree of social order.[16] But not even this is sufficient. Feudal society justifies its distribution of property by reference to the requirements of its defense.[17] The possession of property is equated with martial duty and capacity, each man holding what he is demonstrably both required and able to defend. Authority, then, verges on the stage of nature. Its possessors are threatened with tenures that are "solitary, poor, nasty, brutish, and short." Failure is equated with illegitimacy. The naked fact of dispossession brooks no argument.

For a stable social order, criteria other than military are clearly necessary. An internal dominant elite must, if it is to stability, secure individual members in the possession of the status and property they have acquired. Agreement among its own members must legitimize the existing arrangement of holdings. The collective body must consider itself attacked when any one of its members is dispossessed.

To the extent that an internal dominant system is successfully established, the status of its members must be threatened neither by war nor by internecine rivalry. The dominant position of the feudal elite is guaranteed as long as they retain their arms-bearing monopoly. Defeat, local or general, may overthrow a particular set of holdings; membership in the chivalric order, however, should ensure even the dispossessed of a superior status. Given the right to bear arms, it is assumed that the other possessions will follow.[18] It is in those who, in themselves and in their ancestors, "have always been submitted to servitude" that the danger lies—in the acquisition of property and authority by individuals excluded from or hostile to the chivalric order.

The blood-elite self-image of the internal dominant elite divides their society sharply into two nonassimilable classes. Pride of descent is, in general, ambitious rather than pious. The hazy contention that none of his ancestors was a slave may exist in the mind of the feudal lord, but it pales before the strength of his determination that his descendants shall be at least as powerful as he. Considerations of security demand that the feudal elite as a class evolve a common policy determining the possession and transmission of property. If the conquered areas represent a state of nature to external dominant elites, one to be exploited for the benefit of the "civilized" community, the possessions of the internal dominant elites represent the basis of the personal power and the guarantee of the social order inherent in each member of the caste.[19]

Feudal security, then, depends upon the firm adherence to a *social model* of a two-class society. Authority, the right of property, and military skill are the characteristics of one sharply defined group; their absence, the attribute of the other. Factors limiting any one of this trinity automatically affect the others in equivalent degree. The delegation of authority carries with it the right and the necessity of bearing arms and of holding property, and, since these are the exclusive characteristics of the military elite, entrance into the ruling class. Authority cannot, therefore, be entrusted to mere policy instruments chosen from outside the ranks of the feudal elite. Its exercise involves the personal possession of other characteristics which, taken in a bloc, serve to identify the naturally elect.

This peerage of arms-bearing and property is, however, receptive to gradations of status and degree. Feudal lords have attributes which distinguish them qualitatively from everyone else. Within the elite, however, these attributes admit of quantitative measurement. Their distribution provides a means for centralized controls. In particular, it is land, the most tangible factor, which provides a measure for distinction and subordination within the ruling class. The ability of the sovereign to distribute and redistribute land is one and the same as his power to confer and withdraw status. The legitimization of authority, the nonservile pedigree, and the right to bear arms flow in turn from status so conferred.

This circular process generates the instability of feudal government. Expertly aggressive feudatories use their authority to extort an equivalent measure of status from their suzerain. Ineptly aggressive ones are penalized in status for their inability to defend their possessions. Ideally, the authority of the sovereign should operate through the translation of his superiority in property, martial prowess, and pedigree into a capacity to transfer status and property to his followers. The limits of his control within an internal dominant system are to be sought in the distribution of such items.

Balancing this contest for status are the ties which a common chivalric code produces among the competitors. Members of an internal dominant elite are dependent on one another for recognition and support in the vital matter of self-identification in their exalted role. The existence of the feudal warrior begins and ends within the limits of his own internal dominant military structure. Unlike external dominance, internal dominance provides no metropolitan base from which a candidate may set forth, accredited although as yet unproved. His credentials are entirely in the possession of the body of his peers.

Internal dominant elite candidates must, in response to this circumstance, establish themselves through caste competition. The rites of initiation take the form of a series of trials which test the aspirant's ability to uphold and adhere to the common code. A complex apparatus of vigils, jousts, tourneys, liege obligations, etc., all stressing the common links of a morally and martially competent class, thus comes into being. The competition naturally underlying the system is formally transformed into a declaration of mutual admiration; aggressive impulses, into an affirmation of fraternity.[20]

Closed Equality

Military organization on the structure of *closed equality* characterizes a social system whose nonmilitary parts have grown in power and complexity to the point of being able to challenge the power of the military elite. In schematic terms, it represents a situation where military command, though still the undisputed monopoly of the military elite, has been subordinated to the problem of administering the general social order. In pursuit of this objective, nonmilitary groups gain possession of vital sections of the decision-making apparatus.

The word "equality," here employed, refers to the transformation of political responsibility from possession into privilege. In the "dominant" type of society such responsibility is indistinguishable from military authority; the nonmilitary are by that very condition excluded from any participation in the affairs of the state. A dominant society does not possess a unifying concept such as citizenship or nationality. Its members are described by the terms that divide them, the simple antinomy of rulers and ruled. In the "equality" type of society, on the other hand, political responsibility is a privilege open to all inhabitants, at the discretion of the sovereign. As natives, they are all equal in his eyes. Whatever distinctions and privileges they may achieve stem from his judgment of how well they have served him.[21] This is not to say that "equality" is egalitarian. The privileges bestowed come in the form of a gift, not a right; since they are the ruler's fiat, they clothe social distinctions with the sanctity of law. This law operates through a single judicial system which incarnates the sovereign personality and which takes the entire population under its jurisdiction. Extraterritoriality and private justice characterize "dominant" social-military relationships; centralized justice and public codes, the "equality" types.

The historical setting of *closed equality* has been the nation-state with its political tradition of indivisible and absolute sovereignty. Political authority, which in feudal society was the balance and sum total of the property holdings of the military elite—the concrete interest and security of a chosen few—is elevated to an abstract entity which transforms the sovereign from an aristocrat primus inter pares into a qualitatively unique being.[22] The destiny and welfare of the society are regarded as being entirely within his hands. The totality of his power is justified by an assertion of the primitive and undifferentiated insecurity of his subjects, of the chaos and anarchy which precede the establishment of the "state."

Status distinctions within the closed equality structure are based on service to the sovereign. Public office, not property or "civilization," is the means and measure of success.[23] Under such a system, nationality, i.e., residence within the territory divinely entrusted to the sovereign authority, and training in warfare and law—the professional skills of public administration—are the major qualifications for preferment. The institutional embodiments of these professional skills take the form of monopolistic and self-perpetuating corporations. As instruments of the commonwealth, they are theoretically open to all citizens. A demonstrated mastery of the professional code and ritual, rather than pedigree or property, is the means of entrance into the office-holding elite.

Closed equality elites are not, however, rootless. The importance given to nationality and professional ethics serves to preserve the connection between property and military authority. Since nationality signifies residence, the possession of landed property is regarded as a demonstration of social commitment; the greatest property holders are the most "resident" and, therefore, the truest members of the state. Morever, since military command is regarded as the most effective means for asserting the sovereign's dignity and authority, landed proprietors, as the subjects most bound to his favor and will, are logically most fit to lead his armies.

Landed property is, in addition, regarded as the most public form of wealth. The sum total of its extent defines the authority of the sovereign. He rules over his dominions and thence over his subjects. His control of their property precedes his control of their lives. Moreover, property is nonfluid and cannot, like bodies, specie, and commodities, be transferred across national boundaries to weaken and impoverish the state. Landed proprietors are therefore the most suitable recipients of the sovereign's confidence. The nature of their fortunes renders them most dependent on him and most subject to his control. The immovability of their wealth stands as a bond for their loyalty to the state. Their self-interest demonstrably requires a rigid professional morality.

Trade and commerce are, therefore, forbidden to the office-holding class. Military leadership, in particular, is restricted to members of the property-holding aristocracy, bred and trained exclusively in this capacity and barred from any other occupation. The condition of closed equality may, for its military leaders, represent a decline from feudal conditions where the army had undisputed control over society. The military pursuit, nevertheless, is still the most honorable public office. Though it may be degraded to some extent by being regarded as an office and thus lumped with other professions, it is still esteemed as the profession theoretically devoted to the most essential portion of well-being of the state. In a closed equality social-military relationship, non-military offices, though publicly rewarded, are regarded as inferior and personally debasing.

On the basis of this assessment of relative social importance, the closed equality military elite create an image of themselves as the nation's heart and brain, the part devoted to the direction and balance of the whole. To emphasize this role, members of the military aristocracy cultivate habits of conspicuous waste and carefully avoid spending their time and energies on anything that may be regarded as directly productive or rewarding. Wealth, when it does come to them, must come in the form of largesse.

This, of course, is not to credit them with an ascetic outlook. Material possessions are regarded by members of this group as indispensable to the maintenance of proper professional standards. It is their belief, however, that the state, in recognition of the vital function they perform, should take steps to provide them with the necessary materials.

This claim on the part of the military to lavish support is not solely based on their estimation of the political value of military service. It is perhaps even more strongly founded on the social function which the military virtues play within the nation-state. In a society where the nominal condition is that of equality, where every man is free to improve his social and material position, regardless of its public consequence, the aristocratic imagination sees "mere anarchy" ever ready to be "loosed upon the world." Commercial enterprise and self-improvement can easily destroy the order and allegiance necessary to good government. The interests of the state are threatened by a turmoil of private and materialistic interests. The devotion to the public interest that is the basis of aristocratic status and privileges stands as the sole safeguard, the indispensable keystone, of an ordered society.

The policy role, then, which the leaders of a closed equality military structure claim for themselves is that of formalizing the dangerously fluid and unstable system of which they form the topmost part, of restricting the influence of the other less nationalized professions, and of playing the vital part of heart or brain—depending upon the current state of anatomical knowledge—amid a mad welter of grasping limbs and engulfing digestive tracts. The military calling, with its absolute dissociation from all forms of commerce, trade, and other international interests, stands as an assurance that the most vital of public offices will not be open to anyone whose devotion to the state might be called into question. By virtue of its position at the head of the social hierarchy, the army is able to insist, as the first condition of an active public career, that successful members of other professions resign from their original callings and convert their wealth into land. By designating military service as an essential apprenticeship to superior status, it obliges all aspirants to the latter to undergo a prolonged period of aristocratic indoctrination. By insisting and arranging that all members of the ruling class be possessed of a common background and outlook, one which ensures their devotion to and immersion in the service of the state, the closed equality elite claims to preserve its society.

The overall attraction of this organic model lies in this quasi-scientific legitimization of social mobility, in its transformation of status into a form of personal sacrifice. As long as it is possible for "newly arrived" wealth to be converted into land, and for private success to purchase public office, the suppression of individual ambition and class claims and the pursuit of national harmony correspond to the justification of the status quo.[24] The problem of converting political or economic prosperity into social status is thereby simplified. The social model of a closed equality structure is a state where self-betterment is linked to public office and where the officially recognized and therefore publicly oriented professions have the ascendency in prestige, wealth, and power over privately oriented ones. The social doctrines of an organic classless society assert that the political strength of the nation is the prior and necessary condition for the personal well-being of its members. The professions devoted to that strength therefore deserve special privileges and rewards.

In the military sphere, then, commissioned rank is, on a primitive level, regulated through a purchase system, operating on the hypothesis that the supremacy of the military elite is so firmly established that it is impossible for anyone to possess the necessary wealth without having qualified, in some more essential way, for membership. As the dominance of the landed aristocracy is reduced, however, it becomes necessary to establish some means of distinguishing officers whose presence represents the power of the lower professions from those who are the true representatives of the "born and bred" soldier. In this advanced form, the role concept of the military elite in a closed equality type of society takes the concrete shape of a general staff. There the military aristocracy is entrusted with planning for the defense of the nation; the actual fighting is left to the parvenus. Functionally speaking, this new responsibility involves a shift in professional emphasis from personal valor to logistic and strategic proficiency. The mission of the military elite is to organize and direct the national military establishment. Its position as the exemplar of dynamic leadership and martial virtues, personal rather than official qualities, is merely a ceremonial one.

The emergence of the staff concept implies a general weakening of elite control. The inability to impose aristocratic standards on the totality of the officer corps is paralleled by the disappearance of a free hand in the enrolling of recruits. As the notion of civic responsibility filters down through society, increasing numbers of the general population claim exemption from what is for them service in a particular area. To the degree that aristocratic background is equated with planning capacity, limits are imposed on the autonomy of the military elite. In recruiting its enlisted personnel, it is obliged to seek the cooperation of other high status groups, i.e., professional and entrepreneurial elites.[25] The army, as part of an organic state, is drawn from the body of the population, according to a national consensus about the rights and obligations of military service. Those of the nonmilitary already acknowledged to be performing a public service are considered exempt—conscription is, therefore, the proclamation of a private, i.e., nonprivileged, status. In a closed equality society, the great social-military debate centers on the nature and the extent of the conscription laws.

The drafting of conscription laws reaches beyond the personnel needs of the national military establishments. It represents, in explicit terms, the relationship of groups other than military to the state. Since, according to the principle of organic differentiation, military service is unnatural for all but the military elite, it is generally regarded as a burden and an imposition. The claims of other professions to useful public service demand recognition in the form of exemptions for their members. Ideally, citizens should be conscripted to the extent that their professions are devoid of public utility. The fact of conscription does then imply a social rebuke. The enlisted core of a peacetime establishment is presumed to consist of those citizens whose lives are otherwise entirely useless.[26] In time of war, these are supplemented by drafts of those whose nonmobilized efforts represent a marginal social contribution.

As is to be expected, every occupational group will employ its political power and prestige to render itself exempt from military service. The relations between the military elite and the rest of the nation therefore resolve themselves into a series of maneuvers where each group attempts to bring about the arrangement of military service most favorable and flattering to its members, and where the military seek to gain the greatest possible degree of freedom in filling their enlisted ranks. Once the need for a large national army or militia has been accepted—national armies and militias as the sovereign image of a nation's might are almost always large—the military elite is driven to come to terms with the most influential nonmilitary groups. The alliance thus formed secures the enactment of the necessary conscription legislation. The actual process of bargaining constitutes the machinery of civilian control. The military may be considered independent within the state only insofar as they are free from the necessity of dickering with nonmilitary groups over conscription.

The independence of armies is not, however, a simple matter of national compliance. It involves the willingness of the total society to allow the military to assume what they consider to be their natural role and form. In a social structure of closed equality, military organization fosters a sense of proprietary autonomy on the part of its elite. Though they are dependent on the rest of society for their material, the army is personally theirs. Its direction is a caste monopoly. Its units are the property of the assigned commanders.[27] In the eyes of military leaders, then, civilian consultation is a specimen of organic disequilibrium which forces the army to relinquish a portion of its rightful powers and which brings private interests to bear on what is, in essence, a public trust.

The sanctity of office expressed in a military authority and organization is a vital component of the aristocratic monopoly of military leadership. Since the regiment is the official responsibility of its commander, the appointment of its officers is entirely up to him. The public safety is endangered if parties other than his sovereign question his handling of it. The authority he is delegated empowers him to select his officers free from private pressures.

The acceptability of an officer recruit is thus ensured by making his appointment a sinecure of senior caste members. Military units have their charter in the privileges granted to such officers to raise them, not in the functional subdivision of the national force. As a result, military prestige within a closed equality structure centers on the traditions and the status of individual regiments. Emulation within the system takes the form of a competition among regiments for "guards" status, i.e., an intimate connection with the person of the sovereign, and of an effort among officers to incorporate this status into their personal bearing and behavior. The occupational ambitions of the officer recruit focus on securing admission to a distinguished regiment,[28] rather than on acquiring technical martial proficiency, the respect of his fellow officers, or the devotion of his enlisted men. The latter considerations are not excluded, but they are secondary in importance.

As a result, the aristocratic officer operates within a closed system, one centering on the values of its senior members. In a more positive sense, the individual operational units of the military organization claim an ethical foundation for themselves, a professional standard which they profess to find lacking outside their particular regimental bounds; even other regiments may be beyond the pale. The exercise of aristocratic virtues is restricted to the regimental mess and parade ground and has neither meaning nor recognition beyond them. The active, aristocratic life can be pursued only in the company and under the approving gaze of one's fellow officers. Apart from the good society of the proper regiment, there is only an individualistic, plebeian solitude.

Open Equality

Military organization on the structure of *open equality* characterizes a social system in which a clear-cut and officially recognized hierarchy of professions is no longer an article of faith. Within such a system, the exclusive measure of distinction is technical proficiency in any given field, as judged by success on the open market. It is a world in which a path is naturally, indeed almost automatically, beaten to the doorstep of the builder of bigger and better mousetraps.[29]

The social structure embodied in an open equality army claims to be practical rather than ideal. Closed equality systems measure the utility of individual citizens by the nature of their official involvement. An open equality social system, on the other hand, regards all citizens as publicly useful on the basis of their private interests. Success in the pursuit of such interests is regarded a valid index of public responsibility.[30]

The policy base of an open equality structure is founded on the belief that all privately useful skills are politically useful. It rests, therefore, on what it considers to be a representative society, one which distributes its authority according to the broad patterns of demonstrated enterprise and success. Its military system reflects this prejudice and favors careerists whose skills are readily translatable into aptitudes considered desirable by the general social system. The pay scale of private enterprise is mirrored in the classification of military specialties.

The military self-image of an open equality representative system claims for itself the same qualities of expertise and technical proficiency that are used to justify distinctions within the general managerial elite. Leadership comes to be vested in the hands of the expert according to the assessed value of his expertise. The military technician is favored over the rounded aristocrat whose advancement is determined by his demonstrated loyalty to his caste and his mastery of its customs. The open equality technician's career is regulated by his demonstrated devotion to his instruments and mastery of their mechanical peculiarities.[31]

Since the expertise is determined by a "progressive" social outlook, the open equality military elite are likely to have many of the qualities of a "man on the make." Guided by a desire to gain the maximum utility from the machines and manpower at their disposal, they are inclined to employ these items according to the prevalent managerial standards rather than to force them into the mold of military code and traditions.

As an expert openly competing with other experts, the military leader tends to evaluate himself in terms of the general society, an evaluation intensified by the willingness of that society to reward him on such terms. Generals of armies are assumed to be interchangeable with captains of industry, and the transitions are relatively frequent—from the military to the industry in peacetime and from industry to the military in wartime. The soldier is expected to demonstrate that he is an economically viable item. His rewards are modeled on those of private industry.

The desire to be recognized as a legitimate enterprise leads the armed forces to adopt the policy role of "embodying" the industrial principles and know-how of society, of presenting themselves as the culmination of many autonomous lines of entrepreneurial development. "Learn a trade" and "Travel, Education, Security, Career" are advertised inducements for long-term military service. In the provision of equality of opportunity and openness of career, open equality armies strive to be more civilian than civil society itself.[32]

The social model of an open equality military structure is that of entrepreneurial classlessness, a society in which all members are privately oriented and where the pursuit of particularized ingenuities results in the common welfare. The entrepreneurial classless military officer differs from the organic classless one in that he no longer regards himself either as the proprietor of his command or as the conscience of his state. His self-image is that of the operator of the machinery of national defense. It is not that this conscience and proprietorship have been usurped by some other occupational group; rather, the standards of technical efficiency which uniformly motivate all citizens have eliminated the need for an architectonic element and can be depended upon to ensure the common security.[33]

Members of this military elite see themselves as matching other enterprising citizens in efficiency and as managing a military machine which exploits to the fullest the available manpower and techniques. Since they no longer lead their society, they are not responsible for determining the moment and direction of war. They are responsible only for being in readiness when it does occur. Hence the paradox of the essentially passive military leaders of an open equality army whose duty it is to draft detailed war plans against any conceivable opponent, while the more active closed equality force can restrict its planning to a predetermined foe.[34]

In effect, the technological orientation of the open equality military officer restricts his share of the responsibility for the national defense. He does not claim to be a member of a caste morally qualified for leadership. Instead, the open equality expert regards himself as a martially oriented member of the general body of managerial technicians. His commission is based on acquired skills. The scope of his responsibility is determined by the technological and operational importance attached to the instruments of which he is the acknowledged expert. His military competence ceases simultaneously with his expertise.[35] Policy is determined by a consensus of the informed, rather than by the conscience of the elect.

Since military authority is dependent on the technical and operational capabilities of the instruments entrusted to it, power struggles among the military tend to center on the allotment and development of new technological instruments and of new technologically oriented missions. Established military branches claim priority in the development and organization of these roles and strive to present the new instruments as logical developments of those they already possess.

Thus the general social system, as the sum total and final arbiter of technical competence, has firm control over the operations and the organization of its military component. Since it is the accepted judge of technical capabilities, it can allot the responsibility for weapons research and development among the various military branches. A branch slighted or ignored in this technological race faces the immediate prospect of a decline in prestige and activity and the eventual one of obsolescence. Its survival comes to depend on its ability, not to develop professional self-sufficiency, but to present itself as a microcosm of the social whole. The evaluation of technological capacity, under an open equality military structure, is the index of success; and since the criteria of such an evaluation are expressed in civilian terms, the machinery of their application provides an effective instrument of civilian control.

Within the military organization the predominance of techno-logical criteria takes the form of an extreme rivalry among the various component branches. The orientation of individual officers is determined by the weapons systems they service. Here, competi-tion is not only among army, navy, and air force, but also among the components of these branches, tactical air versus strategic air, armor versus infantry, submarines versus carriers.[36]

Such branch rivalry serves as an instrument of officer candidate indoctrination. The command aspirant is imbued with the belief that his chosen or assigned branch is militarily the most important, in the sense that its technological contribution is either the most far-reaching or the least subject to obsolescence. The vital mission of each branch is put forth as a claim to the highest priority in the control and the development of new weapons. The service of its particular weapons and techniques is asserted to require a higher level of technological competence and a more progressive outlook than those of any other military branch.

Their training as candidates likewise tends to make officers creatures of the branch they have entered. Particular military aptitudes find recognition and reward only if the unique contribu-tion of their assigned arm is publicly recognized and encouraged. As specialists, officers become the victims of an early military marriage, which narrowly limits the range of their future assign-ments. Their general social standing as productive members of the commonwealth intimately depends on the technological evalua-tion of the service to which they belong. The responsibility of his actual assignment and the prospects of his long-range career lead the open equality officer to fuse his interests with those of his assigned branch and to regard members of other services as person-al and technical obstacles.

Ideological Equality

Military organization in the structure of *ideological equality* characterizes a social-military relationship in which the distribution of power and authority is determined by individual display of doctrinal commitment. In more concrete terms, it represents a situation where the "party" regards itself as the synthesis and suppression of both society and state,[37] and where the degree of active adherence to the party program and dogma is the measure not only of status and authority but also of membership in the community itself.

The policy base in all aspects, including the military, of an ideological equality structure is the totalitarian community. In such a community, activity or belief at variance with the party doctrine is treason. The totalitarian community demands the fullest possible participation by its members in public affairs on the grounds that its program encompasses all legitimate aims and occupations; all unassimilated organizations, internal or external, are therefore enemies.

The equality of totalitarian ideology is based on a dogmatic refusal to give any weight to private capacities of judgment and decision. The official doctrine has the sanctity of the ideal and the inevitable. Individual insights are imperfect and transient. Private activities, no matter how momentarily beneficial to the general welfare, represent a lower level of knowledge. As such they are personally harmful and deprive individual members of that possibility of salvation which it is the function of the community to insure. Under ideological equality, individual capacities do not exist; the power to act is a reflection of adherence to dogma. All adherents are, as such, equal.

The supreme penalty, therefore, is to be refused the opportunity of party service. Ideological equality draws every citizen into the service of the militant faith.[38] Only those who are considered incapable of belief are exempted.[39] Since belief is salvation, the excluded are damned.

In such an environment, military rank is an official index of militant belief.[40] The structures of party, army, and state coincide.

Rank is distributed according to the degree that the individual assimilates the official ideology into his attitudes and behavior; insubordination is defined as a display of independent personal existence.

The self-image of ideological equality leadership is that of charisma.[41] The leader is the personification of the outlook and aspirations of his ideological following, the mouthpiece of the doctrine in action. As a "natural" leader and the incarnation of the faith, the member of the ideological equality elite contrasts most sharply with the open equality expert. The latter's authority is dependent on some external display, the mastery of some objective instrument or technique. It is possible, therefore, for such an expert to survive operational disasters, provided that he can convince his political superiors that failure was caused not by his technical incompetence but rather by the lack of the necessary instruments or by restrictions on his use of them.[42]

Failure, on the other hand, is inadmissible for the ideological equality leader. His competence and his authority must find their complete expression within the limits of his command. Since he is assumed to be the personification of a specific collective will, he must be a figure of undiluted omnipotence. The military leader as a charismatic figure is committed to success.[43] The validity of a belief and the legitimacy of a community hang on his career. Defeat, rather than a jeopardizing of the authority of the party and its beliefs (these two are considered identical), puts into question the validity of the leader's claims.[44]

The ideological equality leader, as the voice and the incarnation of the community he heads, assumes full responsibility for its welfare. Since the accepted faith demands unanimity of belief and uniformity of behavior, the definition and enforcement of orthodoxy are a leadership function. The presence of the nonbeliever and the nonparticipant is regarded as a hostile act, and it is one of the leader's duties to unmask and expel such individuals. True believers living outside the community are also his responsibility. It is the duty of the leader to enable them to live according to the fullness of the true faith. They are, therefore, regarded as fellow communicants imploring acceptance and support by the totalitarian community. True leadership involves the recognition of the right of such petitioners to practice their beliefs openly and fully, and the willingness and capacity to bring this about.

The policy role of an ideological equality military organization is that of propagation—of extending the active application of the ideology so as to include all of its valid adherents. The latter are regarded as persecuted, insofar as any part of their daily existence falls outside of the millenarian pattern of the party program. A community formed in the pattern of ideological equality is therefore a revolutionary and expanding one. It lends its support to all who adhere to its creed and regards with hostility all those remaining uncovered. To the extent that it has borders, it is aggressive; and to the extent that it is aggressive, it sharpens its own ideological self-consciousness.

For an ideological equality army, therefore, inherited boundaries and international conventions have no validity. Established political norms are discarded in favor of the immediate possibilities of militant action. A community dedicated to the attainment of its particular beatitude cannot consider itself bound by limitations stemming from the imperfect perceptions of unregenerate societies. Its actions are governed by the belief that only to it has the vision of a perfect community been given, and it has in that way been set apart from and over its neighbors. The process of organizing the ideal social order is inseparable from that of expanding it to the fullness of its perfection.

The army of ideological equality structure regards itself as the assembly of true believers. Its social model is a communal one: the open and equal association of all those who are brethren in faith.[45] This equalitarianism is strengthened by the belief that, insofar as the ideology is true, it is rational, and, insofar as man is a social animal, natural. The acts of the community, including warfare, are constructive and necessary. As opposed to the destructive, irrational, and oppressive acts of nontotalitarian societies, totalitarian warfare is a force for education and public welfare.

Ideological equality mobilization is, on that account, total. The ranks of a closed equality military structure are in wartime filled out by those whose normal contribution to the society justifies a demand for extra service. Submarginal contributors in peacetime are obliged to pay for their membership in the commonwealth with a supplement of military duty. In an open equality structure, the enlisted ranks are filled by those whose technological relationship to society makes their contribution a necessity. As the normal and necessary constituents of any representative peacetime operation, their presence in the military machine is an essential guarantee of its effective operation. In an army of the ideological equality structure, however, the unqualified drafting of the entire community is an assertion both of the justness of war and of the solidarity of its support. The full participation of the faithful is an unquestionable proof of the community's virtue.

The role of "social model" given to the concept of "community" stems from the belief that the individual is a member to the degree that his personal traits incorporate the dominant ideology. Personality is acceptable only as a form of collective expression. On this basis, equality admits of gradation: "some men are more equal than others," that is, they represent progressively broader sections of the community. The gamut of community participation extends from those who barely escape being eliminated as "enemies of the people" to those who stand out as the very incarnation of the people.

It follows that there is a premium on expressing personal motivations in policy terms. Conversely, once a policy has been officially adopted, members of the community are immediately obliged to accept it as a natural part of their character structure. [46] The declaration of war, then, assumes that all true believers are natural soldiers, already enrolled in their proper ranks, and that the army is an abstract term describing the total community engaged in an unavoidable act of self-expression and self-fulfillment.

Acts of war, like all other acts in a totalitarian community, are regarded as a natural expression of the common will. Leaders are accordingly regarded as a manifestation of that popular and invariably correct entity. Every command incorporates its proper slice of faith and reality. The two are, in fact, equated. The true commander is the successful one. The problem of centralized control is, then, difficult. Even if the highest leaders immediately assume the formal and personal command of all operations, there yet remains the problem of maintaining ascendancy over commanders whose authority is also assumed to be based on an inner voice which inevitably grows louder to the degree that they are successful.

Totalitarian movements harbor a strong antinomian component, particularly in their military aspects. True leadership is often regarded as the antithesis of conventional military procedures. The subjective requirements of the community are closer to reality than the objective science of the detached observer. A leader establishes himself as "natural" by demonstrating his ability to disregard and abolish professional restraints. Consequently, any attempt to "regularize" military command and to subject it to some sort of coordinating control is regarded as a plot to undermine the leader's claim to authority and to destroy the basis of his ascendancy. Centralized authority may come to represent a force actively and blindly opposed to the will and experience of those actually engaged in the struggle.[47]

The ultimate resource of "high" command in such a situation is to take advantage of the personalized and clear-cut distinctions among its armed forces and to balance one group against another. Necessity, like equality, can, in a totalitarian context, admit of degree. All campaigns are vital to the state. Some, nevertheless, are more vital than others; they become decisive. Failure, of course, discredits a leader, particularly a subordinate one. Success in a given area, on the other hand, may be controlled by the official reevaluation given to his campaigns.[48] This process will involve a reassessment of past campaigns and a general proclamation of the crucial points and decisive moments. As an instrument of analysis and of direct inference, the study of the past is essential to the waging of ideological controversy; the process of controlling a totalitarian elite involves writing and rewriting official history. The contribution of favored leaders or their precursors is stressed, that of their unsuccessful rivals minimized or denied.[49]

The head of the totalitarian state, as the incarnation and the mouthpiece of common truth and knowledge, is in a position to control the authority and prestige of his subordinates. Possessing the power to define the ideology, both as dogma and as experience, he is in a position to determine the "real" importance of the achievements of the various communal subgroups. Effective participation, and consequently power, in the communal effort depend on the kind of recognition the superme leader is willing to give.

Indoctrination within an ideological equality military structure is therefore carried out in terms of the organizational entities with the closest relationship to the ideological objectives of the war, its operational fronts, and the armies assigned to them. These units are designated according to the area which it is their mission to liberate or defend: Leningrad Group, Army of the Rhine, etc. In much the same manner as citizens identify themselves with their communities and their leaders, ideological equality · soldiers identify themselves with their operational units and their commanders.[50]

The prestige of particular armies and particular operational fronts is thus the key factor in the integration of citizens into their military units. Theoretically an ideological army lacks a command elite.[51] As true believers, its soldiers are already members of the elect. The community does not recognize specialists. For it, only the faithful exist. Distinctions of command are assumed to mark degrees of communal participation, not of professional aptitude.[52] The orthodoxy and, therefore, the reward, of a particular army are equated with the role of its leaders in the official account of the victories gained.

It is thus to the interest of every "follower" that the prestige and authority of his leader increase. Charismatic appeal translates itself into a political machine whose operator advertises his talents and achievements in order to attract and hold the most brilliant possible conglomerate of subordinates. The careers of the latter are indissolubly joined to his, and they acquire honors in the degree that the leader's fame and authority spread.[53]

Rivalry in this process is thus among competing leaders. External threats touch only on the general welfare; individual careers are determined by internal events. The personal threat comes from competing corporate segments within; in the case of the military, from rival armies. Subordinates in the category of ideological equality have greater fear of domestic denunciation than of enemy action. The violence of their efforts to remain aligned and identified with the orthodox dictum creates the dynamics of both the expansion and the dissolution of the totalitarian order.[54]

CONCLUSIONS

The five types here described are meant to represent states of mind. It is not claimed that they correspond to actual organizational structures. They are states of mind equally open to soldier and civilian. The military seek to promote social traits guaranteeing themselves organizational and operational stability, while civilians look for military standards which ensure them an army which will guard, not undermine, their society.

The pure type is, of course, a tool of the theorist. Its construction can proceed independently of the anachronisms and traditions which color the outlook of the martially and civilly committed and which enable both to operate more or less effectively and simultaneously at several structural levels. An air power enthusiast may carry a swagger stick into the cockpit, while the advocate of a professional military "brain" may put it to work on plans based exclusively on the offensive spirit and elan. Colonial powers such as France and Great Britain may maintain two kinds of armies, different in both organization and outlook, one for the homeland and the other for overseas possessions. Competing service arms may attach themselves to conflicting social traditions. Such disparities are part of the description which precedes and illuminates analysis.

The analysis of such particulars may, moreover, by indicating areas where a conceptual strain exists, be helpful in the study of conflicts within military forces as well as those between civil and military authority. Political stability presupposes a general consensus among elites about the role and composition they assume— military effectiveness, a general acknowledgment of the necessity of the broad features of doctrinal and disciplinary control. When through inherent contradiction or incomprehension these fail, when the legitimacy of leadership is denied, or when the means and instruments of maintaining it are withheld, the alternatives are likely to be mutiny, sedition, and revolt; within the organization, against the organization, or in the extreme setting of a civil war.

As to the theoretical implications of the described types, two final points may be made, one concerning their historical relevance, the other concerning their social function. The structures here analyzed are all ideal. The sequence adopted is rational, moving in descending order from the conditions under which formal military organizations have the most active role to those under which they have the least. The types of *external dominance* and of *ideological equality* represent the poles of social-military relationships. External dominance describes a situation in which all policy norms and relations are based on needs and practices which are military in the most narrow sense; ideological equality, one in which all decisions flow from the needs and beliefs of the general and undifferentiated society. Both agree in refusing to recognize the rights of outsiders; the nonmilitary in one case and the noncommunal in the other. In the sense of Stoic natural law, then, they are equally without justice. For, to paraphrase St. Augustine: "What are imperial armies but small totalitarian communities? And what are totalitarian communities but great armies?"[55]

Historically, *external dominance* theories have come into being when an ideological equality community has acquired a greater number of undesirable inhabitants than it can conveniently liquidate, when the sheer weight of numbers has made it impossible for the community of true belief to keep itself pure.[56] Accordingly, it has reorganized itself from the nation-in-arms into the civilizing imperial army; the totalizing ideology has become the higher civilization, the socially nondesirable have become members of an officially inferior class.[57] With the broadening of political representation, the structure of military organization penetrates further down the social scale. A theory of social-military evolution may possibly be found in this.

The concept of a military organization as a pure type is also important as a source of social data. Organizational standards enter into the military climate of opinion as a means toward providing an intellectual and emotional setting for the elite, one consistent with their environment and aspirations. Translated into terms of morale, they become ideals and stress aspects of military service considered to be either traditionally or currently glorious. The social and political roles of an armed force are inherent in them.

The disparity between the ideal and the actual in military types may, then, be utilized in the examination of conflicts between military organizations and their social environment. The differences between the role concepts adopted by a given military group and those assigned to it by the overall social structure can serve as the basis for the determination of political realities and conflicts. In much the same manner as the stability of a social system can be described in terms of the acceptance of its ideals among its various component institutions,[58] the ideals of particular institutions, in this case the military, can be defined and examined for the sense in which they both reflect and express the values of their social setting. Conflicts can thus be determined not only in terms of the failure of the sovereign authority to fit a vital governing instrument into the pattern of its particular objectives, but also in terms of the existence within such instrumental organizations of a system of ends and objectives at variance with or in opposition to those of the established order.

Lastly, the application of military ideal types to military actualities may shed some light on military policy at those points where it enters the realm of political controversy. The relations between the potentialities of technique and the actuality of organization may thus be explained in a manner illustrating their applicability to specific objectives and situations, the limitations of specific military systems examined in terms of their necessary roles and missions, and policies involving the use of military organizations judged in terms of the capabilities of the available resources.

The states of mind encompassed by various types of armies, while never perhaps so systematic as the scheme here attempted, can be regarded as an integral part of the military as a functional system. For the purposes of social theory, they may be considered as forming the heart of that morale and opinion which so supreme a military dramatist as Napoleon regarded and demonstrated as making up the better part of the simulacrum of government and of the reality of war.[59]

NOTES

1. The consequences of this absence can be economic as well as political. In a society deprived of external objectives, politics and economics both are reorganized on a local subsistence level. See H. Pirenne, *Medieval Cities* (Garden City, N.Y.: Doubleday, 1956), p. 36. Conversely, failure—for example, the crusader kingdoms—to surmount a form of social and economic organization designed for local self-subsistence makes concerted action against an external threat impossible. See R. C. Smail, *Crusading Warfare* (Cambridge: At the University Press, 1956), pp. 187 ff.
2. Compare the objectives of military groups with those of organizations such as the AFL-CIO or NAM. The latter emphasize the importance of the security and well-being of individual members; the former, the effectiveness of the corporate body.
3. This is not to say that all nonmilitary groups are strongholds of individualism, and that armies are unique in striving to construct a total environment for their members. Military organizations are here considered as exceptionally explicit and well articulated examples of what have been termed "total institutions." See E. Goffman, "On the Characteristics of Total Institutions," *Asylums* (Garden City, N.Y.: Doubleday Anchor, 1961), pp. 1-124.
4. J. L. Talmon, *The Origins of Totalitarian Democracy* (London: Secker & Warburg, 1952), p. 11.
5. The word "elite" is employed throughout in a purely descriptive sense, referring to those who are in formal possession of positions of authority.
6. The colonial use of the word "native" is here ironically suggestive. Indigenous populations are considered as one of the undeveloped natural resources.
7. "Created by wars that require it, the machine now created the wars it required." J. Schumpeter, *Imperialism: Social Classes* (New York: Meridian, 1955), p. 25.
8. "In order to exhibit a continual trend towards imperialism, a people must not live on—or at least not be absorbed by—its own labor. When that happens, the instincts of conquest are completely submerged in the economic concerns of the day." Ibid., p. 46.
9. See, for example, P. Heidsieck, ed., *Rayonnement de Lyautey* (Paris: Gallimard, 1947), pp. 119-200.
10. See Caesar's *Commentaries*, where he consistently presents his actions as the almost unpremeditated consequences of a simple civilizing mission and contrasts them with the political schemes of his opponents, barbarian and Roman.
11. See Alfred de Vigny, *The Military Necessity*, a eulogy of one age of imperial expansion and a prophecy of another.
12. For a description of this process, see J. Masters, *Bugles and a Tiger* (New York: Viking, 1956), in particular pp. 118-124.
13. For an intensive effort to describe and classify feudalism, see Rushton Coulborn, ed., *Feudalism in History* (Princeton, N.J.: Princeton University Press, 1956); in

particular, see R. Coulborn, "A Comparative Study of Feudalism," ibid., pp. 185-395. Professor Coulborn finds feudalism to be a process of social transformation and cultural revival. This chapter's more static approach limits us to the treatment of feudalism as the political expression of an ideal type of social-military relationship. Coulborn's effort to point out broad similarities in the processes of institutional development and cultural change among feudal societies, while offering much illustrative material, does not, therefore, bear directly on the problem approached here.

14. The political and social inadequacy of military virtue is the standard theme of internal dominance romance from Homer to Chaucer.

15. To be noble is to count among one's ancestors no one who has been subjected to servitude. Mon. Germ. LL, T. IV, p. 557, col 2, I 6. Quoted in M. Bloch, *Feudal Society*, trans. L. A. Manyon (Chicago: University of Chicago Press, 1961), p. 286.

16. See J. L. La Monte, *Feudal Monarchy in the Latin Kingdom of Jerusalem, 1100 to 1291* (Cambridge: Cambridge University Press, 1932), pp. 138ff.

17. The border lords of feudal kingdoms, the Mortimers and Percys, invariably received the greatest latitude of means and operations.

18. According to the ideology of feudalism, war is an entrepreneurial activity and looting a legitimate return on the capital outlay represented in armor and equipment. A feudal warrior thus possesses a means to fortune commensurate with his status. See Fritz Redlich, *De Praeda Militari, Looting and Booty 1500-1815* (Wiesbaden: F. Steiner, 1956).

19. "For I do not, Sire, hold that land of Morea either as a paternal or ancestral inheritance, so that I can freely give or grant it away. Those well-born men conquered the land who came with my father hitherto to Romania, as his friends and companions-in-arms. By the sword did they gain the land of Morea, and among themselves they made just distribution of it. To each they gave according to his quality, and thereafter they all chose and made my father, as the man of greatest honor and wisdom among them, leader over all. They set down in written agreements and conventions that he should have no power to make judgment alone, nor indeed to do anything in the world, without the counsel and will of all his companions. And thus, Sire, I am without power to give up anything of the land that I hold, because our fathers gained it by the sword, according to the customs that we hold and that they made in common." *Chronicle of Morea,* ed. J. Schmitt (London: Methuen & Co., 1904), lines 4271-4290.

20. The theme of the brotherhood of all true chivalric warriors is a common feature of the idealization of feudalism; see Americo Castro, "The Presence of the Sultan Suladin in the Romance Literature," Diogenes 8 (autumn 1954): 13-36.

21. See Shakespeare's *Henry V,* a play which can be regarded as a document of emergent national consciousness.

22. See J. Neville Figgis, *The Devine Right of Kings* (Cambridge: Cambridge University Press, 1914).

23. See H. R. Trevor-Roper, *The Gentry 1540-1640* (London and New York: Cambridge University Press, 1953), pp. 34ff.; also Franklin L. Ford, *Robe and the Sword: The Regrouping of the French Aristocracy after Louis XIV* (Cambridge: Harvard University Press, 1953).

24. See Hegel (the classic apologist of this political condition), *The Philosophy of Right,* trans. T. M. Knox (Oxford: Clarendon Press, 1942), p. 197.

25. In an internal dominant system there are, ideally speaking, no enlisted personnel. All fighting men are members of the elite. In an external dominant system, enlisted

personnel are, by definition, excluded from participation in the decision-making processes. See Sales de Bohigas, "Some Opinions on Exemption from Military Service in Nineteenth Century Europe," *Comparative Studies in History and Society* 10 (1967-1968): 261-289

26. "The privates of the American regular army are not the most creditable soldiers in the world; they are chiefly composed of Irish emigrants, Germans, and deserters from the English regiments in Canada. Americans are rare; only those who can find nothing else to do and have to choose between enlistment and starvation, will enter into the American army." Frederick Marryat, *A Diary in America, with Remarks on its Institutions*, 3 vols. (London: Longman, Orme, Brown, Green & Longmans, 1839), 2:305. Commissions in this democratic variant of closed equality were regarded as a form of public office. See S. P. Huntington, *The Soldier and the State* (Cambridge: Belknap Press of Harvard University Press, 1957), pp. 206ff.

27. Down to the reforms of 1871, the British army was a collection of regiments; the regiment was fundamental, whether from the administrative, the social, or the operative standpoint, and was, of course, the property of its colonel. See J. W. Fortescue, *The British Army 1783-1802* (London and New York: Macmillan, 1905), p. 10.

28. See C. Woodham-Smith, *The Reason Why* (New York: Dutton, 1960).

29. "The general prosperity attains a greater height, and is more widely diffused in proportion to the amount and variety of the energies enlisted in promoting it." J. S. Mill, *Utilitarianism: Liberty and Representative Government* (London: J. M. Dent & Sons; New York: Dutton, 1910), p. 208.

30. The famous "what's good for the country is good for General Motors, and vice versa" can be regarded as an expression of faith in the open equality doctrine.

31. The careers of the pioneer air power and armor advocates provide eloquent testimony about the conflict between these two types.

32. It is significant that in the matter of racial desegregation, the U.S. armed forces were obliged to move more rapidly than the rest of American society.

33. In a democratic structure—which we define as one in which power is diffused throughout the society, with no group possessing sufficient power to erect itself into an absolute authority—decision making is decentralized because power is decentralized. See Yale Brozen, "Technological Change, Ideology and Productivity," *Political Science Quarterly* (December 1955), pp. 522-542.

34. In 1914, the German General Staff, the proverbial epitome of military thoroughness, had operational plans only for an attack on France. The nature of their office gave them total responsibility for war. See Gordon Craig, *The Politics of the Prussian Army* (New York and Oxford: Oxford University Press, 1956), p. 294.

35. E.g., the argument that the employment of air power should be solely determined by aeronautical experts; a claim bitterly contested by the old "heart and brain" professional. Similar arguments have been advanced by members of the scientific community concerning the employment of nuclear weapons. The standard *closed equality* argument, on the other hand, is that any technical innovation is just "another weapon" which does not fundamentally alter the nature of war.

36. This rivalry is a feature of the indoctrination of officer candidates. In a closed equality milieu, such as Sandhurst under the former British system, cadets compete for admission into favored regiments—normally the most anachronistic one. In an open equality milieu, such as West Point, cadets compete for admission into the most favored branch, normally the most advanced technological one.

37. See Frederick S. Burin, "Bureaucracy and National Socialism: A Reconsideration of Weberian Theory," in Robert Merton, *Reader in Bureaucracy* (Glencoe, Ill.: Free Press, 1952), pp. 33-47.

38. "The state is all in all. Everything is referred to the production of force; afterwards, everything is trusted to the use of it. It is military in its principles, in its maxims, in its spirit, in all its movements. The state has dominion and conquest for its sole object is dominion over minds by proselytism, over bodies by arms." E. Burke, *The Works of Edmund Burke,* vol. 6, *Letters on a Regicide Peace* (London: George Bell & Sons, 1907), p. 204.

39. Early Bolshevik conscription laws limited military service to "toilers" and those "who do not exploit the labor of another." H. J. Berman and M. Kerner, *Soviet Military Law and Administration* (Cambridge: Harvard University Press, 1955), p. 35.

40. At the outbreak of hostilities, ideological equality leaders put on the uniform and the organizational rank of commander in chief of the armed forces. Open equality leaders merely take on a more intensified exercise of their functions. Cf. Hitler, Stalin, Churchill, and Roosevelt.

41. The word "charisma" is not here employed in the strict Weberian sense of "inner determination and inner restraint" but rather in terms of its political vulgarization. It is the role of the faithful "to provide a following for the dictator with which he can identify himself." So long as it fits the needs and desires of both party and leader, the charismatic illusion, thus invoked, is accepted as a pure and active spiritual force. See Max Weber, *from Max Weber: Essays in Sociology* (New York: Oxford University Press, 1946), pp. 245-250; C. J. Friedrich and Z. K. Brzezinski, *Totalitarian Dictatorship and Autocracy* (Cambridge: Harvard University Press, 1956), pp. 23-26, 29.

42. See the arguments of MacArthur, an ideological equality type leader employed in an open equality setting.

43. "The soldier of the wars of Liberty attached an almost superstitious importance to the carrying out of the smallest order. As a result of this he felt no pity for the generals or officers whom he saw guillotined after a defeat on the charge of dereliction of duty; . . . in his eyes failure could only be explained by some grave error on the part of his leaders. . . . It is not difficult to see that this same spirit is met with in strikes; the beaten workmen are convinced that their failure is due to the base conduct of a few comrades who have not done all that might be expected of them; . . . for the beaten masses, treason alone can explain the defeat of heroic troops; the sentiment, felt by all, of the thoroughness that must be brought to the accomplishment of their duties, will therefore be accompanied by many acts of violence." Georges Sorel, *Reflections on Violence,* trans T. E. Hulme (New York: P. Smith, 1941), p. 289.

44. There is also the possibility that charismatic leaders will assert that their followers have been unworthy.

45. On "spiritual communion" in Nazi and proto-Nazi paramilitary organizations, see R. G. L. Waite, "Vanguard of Nazism," Harvard Historical Studies 60 (1952): 33-57. Also J. Schumpeter, *Imperialism,* pp. 36ff., for the expression of this in early Islam.

46. Soviet Lysenkoist genetics, with its assertion that environment determines character, is a facet of this belief. See Pamela Wrinch, "Science and Politics in USSR: The Genetics Debate," World Politics (July 1951), pp. 486-519.

47. For a direct record of the conflict, see A. S. P. Woodhouse, ed., *Puritanism and Liberty, Being the Army Debates, 1647-9* London: J. M. Dent & Sons, 1938). This is not to assert that Puritanism was totalitarian but only that its *militant* ideology has given rise to certain symptoms of totalitarian conflict.

48. "Membership in the wartime underground, once a badge of courage and honor, has become a stigma in Communist Poland. The heroes of the underground are never mentioned in the Communist Press. . . . The ex-members of the underground are watched by the police and are denied promotion." I. Pool, *Satellite Generals* (Stanford, Calif.: Stanford University Press, 1955), p. 66.

49. See the polemics on the specific civil war contributions of Stalin and Trotsky. Similarly, see the rewriting of World War II history following the death and discreditation of Stalin. B. D. Wolfe, "Operations Rewrite: The Agony of Soviet Historians," Foreign Affairs 31 (October 1952): 39-57.

50. "Just as a peasant would say, 'I am from Ryazan,' a Soviet soldier maintains, 'We are Rodimtzov's boys' or 'Zhukov's boys'; his local patriotism does not extend beyond the boundary of his region or his particular army front." Milhail Koriakov, "The Military Atmosphere," in *The Soviet Army,* ed. B. H. Liddell Hart (London: Weidenfeld, 1956), p. 413. A similar situation existed in the armies of the French Revolution.

51. The abolition of formal rank, or at least of its professional qualifications, is generally one of the first military acts of a totalitarian revolution. The science of war is reformulated in ideological terms. Adherence to the ideology bestows an overall proficiency.

52. "In the meanwhile, the General holds a wolf by the ears; an officer who has seen his troops, about 18,000 men (with a tremendous train of artillery), represents them as a black, daring, desperate crew of buccaneers, rather shocking than contemptible; the officers (scarcely a Gentleman among them), without servants, or horses, or baggage, lying higgledy piggledy on the ground with the common men, yet maintaining a rough kind of discipline over them. They already begin to accuse and even to suspect their General, and call aloud for blood and plunder." Edward Gibbon, *Private Letters of Edward Gibbon,* ed. R. E. Prothero (London: J. Murray, 1896), 2:332; 19 November 1792, re: French Army of the Alps.

53. For example, Napoleon and his marshals, Alexander and his Companions, the attachment of the careers of Voroshilov and Budenny to that of Stalin.

54. For example, the Macedoniam Diadochi, the splits among the successors of Mohammed, Cromwell's major generals, the military leaders of the French Revolution—Hoche, Pichegru, Moreau, Bonaparte.

55. "If there be no justice, what are kingdoms but great robber bands? And what are robber bands but little kingdoms?" Augustine, *The City of God,* 4:40.

56. For two doctrinal efforts in this direction, one attempting to avoid the transformation, the other striving to justify it, see W. W. Tarn, *Alexander the Great* (Boston: Beacon, 1956); V. I. Lenin, *The State and Revolution* (New York: International Publishers, 1932).

57. Macedonia, Islam, Napoleonic France, and Soviet Russia may be taken as examples of this occurrence, and the SS plans for Eastern Europe as an abortive effort.

58. See, for example, Alexis de Tocqueville, *The Old Regime and the French Revolution* (Garden City, N.Y.: Doubleday, 1955), and Friedrich and Brzezinski, *Totalitarian Dictatorship.*

59. Chaplot, ed., *Maximes de guerre et pensées de Napoleon I,* p. 230.

Chapter 3

INFORMATION AND AUTHORITY: THE STRUCTURE

OF MILITARY ORGANIZATION

I

Selfless dedication and inspiring personal example are the polar ideals of the military profession. The trained officer, by selection and indoctrination, is part of an organization that prescribes a rigid model of ends-means calculation and treats human life as simply another material factor. The leader in battle, in contrast, is a member of a caste whose authority is based on the belief that its particular moral qualities dominate the environment and that the inspiration of its particular example can overcome the greatest quantitative odds. The officer is totally sheltered by and thoroughly a creature of the system in which he holds his commission, a system to which he has granted absolute control over his destiny. Yet in situations where fear and indecision represent the common reaction, he is expected to determine the course of events by rising above ordinary behavior and providing a compelling model of resolute and resourceful response.

That military authority has two such aspects is officially recognized. The United States field manual on Leadership draws a distinction between personally acquired authority and formally delegated authority. The former is called *leadership*, the latter

Reprinted from the American Sociological Review, *Volume 24, No. 1, pp. 15-22.*

command.[1] In the interests of the organization, it is essential that the two be harmonized. The initiative undertaken by individuals must conform to the objectives of the group. The designated pattern of collective action must take into account the circumstances and potentialities of the individuals assigned to carry it out.

Such requirements, if elementary, are not simple. The conduct of war imposes an operational gulf between those who plan and those who execute. The high degree of destruction inherent in battle conditions forces those in command to accept certain instances of failure as natural and unavoidable. A calculated probability of destruction and survival dominates the overall picture. Victory is gained in spite of, perhaps because of the failure of, the annihilation of some of the particulars engaged. It is in the essence of the military ethic that weakness at specific points must never be allowed to color an appreciation of the general situation.

It is the particular and the personal, on the other hand, which determine the actions of the executants. In the attainment of local objectives, individuals hope for survival and units seek to maintain themselves as effective and coherent entities. The obstacles to be overcome are those which pose a direct threat to such ambitions.[2]

As a result, the conduct of war progresses along two distinct levels of comprehension. According to the orientation of the "high command," an army represents a self-sufficient system, containing the necessary means for determining and attaining its objectives; the art of planning consists, of course, in balancing these two operations. Enemy opposition in its particular aspects is regarded, therefore, as something falling outside the system—an environmental peculiarity which can be overcome by an appropriate willingness to sacrifice. Enemy opposition must not be allowed to affect the reasoning which enters into the drawing up and the pursuit of the grand design.[3]

Lower-echelon organizations have the dual function of carrying out orders from above and of overcoming local opposition. In the eyes of the high command, the former function is superior to the latter. In the heat of combat, local opposition, nevertheless, is likely to receive the major share of the combatant's attention.

This difference in interest leads to a sharp division as to apprehension and evaluation. High command, with the responsibility of maintaining overall unity in a steady advance toward coordinated objectives, concentrates on maintaining a concerted effort. "Lower leadership," with its survival at stake, concentrates on overcoming a particular threat. Internal order is the concern of one agency; external threats, of the other.

This antinomy of outlooks has found its embodiment in the traditional military opposition of staff and line assignments, differing not only in outlook and objective but also, and even more sharply, in working conditions. The staff setting is that of command. The emphasis given to coordination carries with it a concern for rank and assignment. The chain of command and responsibility is nowhere more clear. Staff men know precisely who their superiors and subordinates are; they also know what is required of them and what sort of assistance they can expect.

The disorganization of combat, on the other hand, strips officers, insofar as they are immersed in it, of their specialized functions. The emphasis under such conditions is not so much upon rationalized individuation as upon group cohesion. Leadership in battle falls to the individual who supplies the convincing example. In uncontrolled circumstances such an example may be one of flight and paralysis; in controlled ones, of resolution and enthusiasm. The leader is not the man who methodically observes the limits and the potentialities of his particular assignment, but the one who establishes his mode of behavior as a meaningful, general norm.

From a functional point of view, then, armies may be regarded as composed of two distinct semiautonomous organizations, each with its particular operational code.[4] Military art (or science) recognizes such a dichotomy in its division of the conduct of war under the two headings of strategy and tactics: the one devoted to the general direction of armies, the other devoted to the particular deployment of men and matériel. Competence in one of these areas has no necessary relation to competence in the other. Military history abounds in generals and actions judged to be strategic failures but tactical successes, or vice versa.

II

When military professionalism is discussed as a modern phenomenon, it is the machinery for strategic decision, the atmosphere of planning, that is emphasized.[5] The armed forces have been accepted as an example of bureaucratic organization. Not only does the general public, for whom every official agency is a bureaucracy, regard them as such, but professional military men consider the bureaucratic model as the necessary setting for the successful conduct of operations. The sociological definition of bureaucracy as "a formal, rationally organized social structure . . . in which, ideally, every series of actions is functionally related to the purposes of the organization"[6] fits the minimal requirements of command.

The form of a bureaucratic, that is, rationally oriented, organization is largely governed by the factors which it believes can be predicted and controlled. Such prediction and control over the movements of their own troops are a matter of commanders' responsibility and faith. If commanders lack these, they cease to command. First emphasis is therefore placed upon the coordination of friendly movements rather than upon the control of hostile ones. The environmental conditions sought by commanders are likely to be those in which their own troops can be most efficiently directed rather than those from which enemy troops may be most effectively observed.

The rational direction of large masses requires planning, and planning requires great stability and calm. The conditions of combat are fluid and haphazard in the extreme. Since disorganization and chance represent a threat, the activities of the organization must be directed toward achieving a working degree of stable and predictable conditions. The exercise of command thus entails a search for enough calm to enable its possessor to rise above the battle.

As a consequence, there is a direct relationship between remoteness from the battlefield and command responsibility: the wider the responsibility, the more remote the post. General officers may, as an incidental part of their duty, spend a good deal of time in the immediate battle area. An occasional visit to the front can serve as a spot check on the reliability of the information guiding headquarters' decisions. It may also be an egalitarian gesture, a concrete demonstration of the commander's belief that the community of fighting men is more important than the formal structure of rank. The command function of planning and coordination, however, is considered to require a sheltered position.

In what is perhaps the most perceptive of all combat studies of World War II, S. L. A. Marshall gives a command analysis by the leader of a highly successful company action.

> "In any such desperate action as a charge, it is necessary to have an officer boldly *leading*. But it is not less important to have one forceful individual remain behind to do the pushing. . . .
>
> "I gave myself the task of remaining behind and prodding them because I am the *commander*. It was my plan and I had given the order. It was my duty to see that it was carried out. I considered that my post should be at the point which offered the best chance of bringing off a successful and complete action."[7]

In other words, this division of labor involves the cultivation of an appropriate point of view. The commander and the leader operate from different positions.

Rank and reason are intimately related. The network of command, moving from high to low, begins with the few invested with the aura of a comprehensive grasp of the situation to be mastered and a knowledge of the principles governing its proper exploitation. It ends with the many whose contact with combat amounts to nothing more than personal experience and who, lacking in and barred from any knowledge of the principles and calculations involved, are expected to do what they are told, and nothing more.[8] In between are those whose position in the command chain determines the mixture of these two roles; more knowledge and less personal experience of battle as they go up, less knowledge and more experience as they go down. The environmental requirements—of command, calm, and freedom from alien disturbances—make it possible to predict the fixed physical position of military officers. As command responsibility increases, the proper station will be progressively to the rear.[9]

III

Such differences in situation result in sharp disagreements in evaluating information. The function of command and the function of leadership, one devoted exclusively to planning and the other to execution, develop their peculiar mysteries. The problems of one remain remote to the other not merely because they are unwitnessed but also because in the context of the assigned task they are devoid of meaning. The fact that one organization is hierarchically superior to the other gives an invidious interpretation to this mutual incomprehensibility. Staff information eludes comprehension because it is esoteric; line information, because it is trivial.[10]

Secrecy has been described as an inherent characteristic of bureaucratic organization.[11] To explain this, the hypothesis has been advanced that the superiority of bureaucratic insiders to nonbureaucratic outsiders is best maintained by excluding outsiders from information about how official decisions are reached. In the general bureaucratic situation, however, those on the outside represent the clients the bureaucrat claims to serve. As such, this public is nonbureaucratic and thereby barred from any intimate association with bureaucratic techniques. But in the special case of military organization, everyone involved is a member of the system and, therefore, party to its operations.

The classic bureaucratic method for dealing with hostile clients is to do nothing for them, to starve them into submission. Then secrecy is a means of maintaining exclusive control over the machinery of administration. In the military sphere, however, the bureaucratic staff exercises its power in giving commands to inferiors. Unless the latter are actively engaged in carrying out orders, the staff itself is inert. The situation among the military is thus reversed. It is in the inactivity of inferiors that the veto threat lies.[12]

With inside authority thus dependent on outside compliance, secrecy cannot be absolute. But since all soldiers are within the system, it is not necessary that the difference be absolute. To combatants, confusion is the essence of war. The need for coordination into a more comprehensive scheme is felt at every level. For his authority to be meaningful, it is only necessary that a superior officer know relatively more.

A captain knows more about what is going on than any lieutenant because he has several lieutenants reporting to him, and so on up the scale. Faith in the military system allows a commander to assume that his subordinates will give him a true picture of the situation before them. The proper performance of this duty allows subordinates to believe that there will be a rational pattern in the orders given to them.

This structuring of information is an integral part of military discipline. Security is not only a precautionary measure, it is also an instrument of authority. It apportions knowledge to rank and thus enables commanders to maintain control over subordinates at times when nothing else responds to their will. Confusion and uncertainty strengthen their hand. In the absence of any other tangible criteria, rank decides. The assertion of superior knowledge and the assertion of authority are often one and the same act. [13]

Because of such considerations, it is clearly desirable that command posts be to the rear. A secluded position protects authority. When the combatant and the commander operate from a common position, the commander's authority is compromised. Commands must then conform to the common experience. Commands obviously based on inaccuracies can destroy official authority.[14]

The decision about whose information is the most accurate amounts to a judgment of the kind of assignments that are the most authoritative. Within the military hierarchy, the type of intelligence possessed by a superior as a superior is by definition considered of a higher order than that available to a subordinate. Consistently, the categories of security classification correspond closely to the degrees of rank.

The establishment of command authority is a circular one. By virtue of his superiority, a superior officer has access to a higher, that is, more relevant and comprehensive, order of information. His directives are to be obeyed by subordinates because of the higher order of knowledge they represent. The maintenance of discipline involves the unwavering assumption that the source of military directives serves as a sufficient warrant of their validity.

Channels of military information thus mirror the chain of command. A subordinate acknowledges his superior not only by carrying out the latter's command but also, since it must be demonstrated that the superior is thoroughly aware of everything going on, by keeping the higher echelons closely informed of the subordinate's movement and situation. To state it simply: the flow of commands is from superior to subordinate, the flow of information from subordinate to superior. A description of the quantity and the direction of these two items normally corresponds to a description of the status structure of the military organization involved.[15]

With role and status so interrelated, certain grave operational difficulties emerge. Information is to be transmitted only along the chain of command. Commanders who are equal in rank or who are members of uncoordinated organizations are under no formal obligation to communicate with one another. Under conditions where units of equal size are fighting side by side, this fact can lead to certain obvious inconveniences. One of the major sources of combat breakdowns cited by Marshall was the ignorance and inertia of commanders about the situation on their flanks, even when front-to-rear communication was in full operation.[16] Lateral communication was virtually nonexistent; the formal structure of command provides no sense of responsibility for such communication. Since the maintenance of close contact with commanders of equal rank was involved, the hypothesis may be advanced that the very nature of military organization inhibited lateral communication. The provision of information might have been regarded as an acknowledgment of subordination.

This last consideration could be declared a fanciful or, at best, a subconscious one were it not for the fact that it plays so prominent a role in the coordination of coalition forces. Where there are two uncoordinated chains of command, considerations of rank and of national autonomy restrict the flow of information between armies. Unless a supreme commander can be agreed upon, each force will prefer to act independently and to regard the provision of detailed operational information to the other as a confession of inferiority. National honor forbids subordination.

Independence and equality of rank are considered incompatible with the unrestricted flow of information.[17]

Access to information, in many ways, takes precedence over formal rank as a determinant of organizational status. The equation of command with planning, and of planning with access to detailed information, can be reversed to give officers with access to detailed information the authority to command. Moreover, bureaucratic specialization can lead to the development of a special corps of officers with the specific assignments of analyzing and reducing to rational order the total body of available information and of drawing up battle plans from the resultant picture.[18] Such a body of officers would have no direct command responsibility. Since command responsibility mirrors official status, specialists are confined to the relatively lower grades.

Access to higher-order information, when officially recognized, can override the claims of formal military rank. An officer belonging to a military section responsible for top-level planning is the ultimate recipient of information. He may thereby acquire authority over officers superior in formal rank whose assignments place them in less intimate contact with the official truth. The legendary function of the Prussian General Staff can be cited as an example of this situation. The high order of information possessed by members of this group empowered them to give directives to officers much superior in grade. On one famous occasion, a General Staff lieutenant colonel ordered an army commander to retreat—a decision which possibly deprived Germany of a chance for quick victory in World War I.[19]

IV

Contact between planners and executants is formally limited to the information the latter transmit to the rear. Information, digested and rationalized, is translated into battle plans. Battle plans are submitted to commanders who break them down into specific concrete decisions and transmit such decisions as orders to the appropriate subordinates. Small wonder, therefore, that a tradition of antipathy has grown up between staff and line officers. In the course of whatever contacts they do have, the former cannot help but appear olympian and the latter all too human.

Attacks within the organization on the effectiveness of higher military authority do not generally concentrate on the quality of the adopted strategy. Lower ranks, through ignorance, are in no position to do so. They stress the kind of information upper echelons do not take into account because of exclusively command preoccupations. The accusation is made that the men at staff headquarters disregard or distort reports coming in from the field[20] and close their minds to any information disturbing their carefully drawn plans. Staff officers are likely to reply that they are motivated by factors far weightier than local considerations— that highly confidential considerations of grand strategy and general policy direct their decisions, which must be carried out whatever the cost, and, in any event, would be meaningless to men on the line.

It is not simply a matter of commanders knowing what is happening at the front. It is a matter of their giving such information a higher priority than the plan of action already decided. The flow of information from front to rear, of course, is an accepted ingredient in the drawing up of the battle picture. The chances are that, by virtue of their authority, higher commanders will restrict this flow to items which they consider to be relevant and which—giving the organizational mind its due—support their plan of action.[21] A tenet of military discipline is that, if the original plan is sound, nothing that occurs in the course of its execution should in any way affect the determination to carry it out. The more professional a military organization regards itself as being, the more strictly it is likely to adhere to this rule of conduct.[22]

An example of such uncompromising military evaluation, all the more interesting for continuing to exist forty years after the event, was given in the commemoration of the battle of Passchendaele in July and October 1917. A commemorative article summed up this action as a tactical failure but a strategic success.[23] The British commander, it was claimed, knew in confidence that the French armies were demoralized and in no condition to face a German offensive, and that unless enemy action were forestalled by the British taking the initiative, the French, and thereby the entire Allied front, were likely to collapse. The British accepted the challenge and gave battle. This decision, although extremely costly in lives, saved the front that year and made victory possible the next.

A series of letters attacked this conclusion. The critics argued that the planning of Passchendaele was carried out in almost total ignorance of the conditions under which the battle had to be fought. No senior officer from the Operations Branch of the General Headquarters, it was claimed, ever set foot (or eyes) on the Passchendaele battlefield during the four months that battle was in progress. Daily reports on the condition of the battlefield were first ignored, then ordered discontinued. Only after the battle did the army chief of staff learn that he had been directing men to advance through a sea of mud.[24]

After forty years of publication and controversy neither side acknowledged the other's point of view. Each side drew up its judgment of the battle to support the claim that its particular experience had provided it with the facts necessary for a correct assessment of the situation. Staff planning was guided by strategic considerations, which were found to consist of the kind of information available and comprehensible exclusively to staffs. Line execution was determined by tactical conditions, which consisted of the situation and predicament of men on the line.

World War I (and this is its utility as a model) represents, for the most part, a situation in which battle was tactically impossible though strategically desirable. Reports from the front, if taken literally, could only have told planners that concerted large-scale action was, for the moment, out of the question.[25] The deadlock enforced by barbed wire and automatic weapons brought about an almost complete dissociation of strategic and tactical thought. Under the circumstances neither could guide the other. It was rather a matter of outright dominance, and the framework of organization gave staff the upper hand.

For planners to take into consideration the tactical conditions would have been an acknowledgment of the superiority of the line's vantage point. The planners would thereby have assigned information coming from the front a higher value than plans formulated in the rear. Line officers, on this basis, would have then been in the possession of the decisive word in the drawing up of plans. Staff officers would have relinquished the superior status and authority given to them by their organizational positions. And of such stuff organization men are not made.[26]

V Summary and Conclusions

Ideally speaking, military operations are painstakingly planned and then carried out with unquestioning resolution. The planning requires conditions of orderliness and calm, the execution creates an environment of disorderliness and confusion. Planners are therefore in the rear; executors constitute in themselves the scene of battle. Differences in assignment result in differences about the point from and the manner in which war is observed. As a result, two antithetical concepts dominate the exercise of military authority.

The professional soldier operates within a bureaucratic framework. Assignments therefore tend to be evaluated according to the scope they provide for rational investigation and orderly procedure. Officers responsible for drawing up plans, then, have higher status than those responsible for their execution. This is so even when the latter are superior in rank.

The superiority of planners is based on the assumption that their position serves to keep them informed about what is happening to the army as a whole, while that of the executors limits their knowledge to personal experience. This assumption is supported by the hierarchical structure of military organization which establishes in specific detail the stages and the direction of the flow of information. In terms of this hierarchy, the man who receives information is superior to the man who transmits it. Since each superior invariably has several subordinates, he enjoys the sum of their information—which, by definition, is greater than any of its parts. By virtue of his position in the organizational structure, the superior is the best informed and, therefore, is best equipped to give orders.

In terms of this same organizational structure, planning, exercise of reason, and rearward position result in high military authority. Execution, dependence on direct personal experience, and frontal position, on the other hand, result in low military authority. The dictates of reason exercised in the rear are, therefore, of greater weight than the facts of experience suffered in the front. Thus plan of operations, once decided, must be carried out even if reports from the scene of combat indicate that it is unrealistic. Determination of this kind is regarded as essential if the military structure of rank and authority is to be preserved.

NOTES

1. "Command is the authority that a member of the military profession lawfully exerts over subordinates by virtue of his rank and assignment. Leadership can be exercised by anyone at any time irrespective of the framework of command." Leadership, FM 22-10 (Washington, D.C.: Department of the Army [March 1951]):3 ff.
2. The occasional circumstance in which death has seemed preferable even to victory represents something other than a military phenomenon.
3. See Karl von Clausewitz, *On War,* trans. O. J. Matthijs Jolles (New York: Modern Library, 1943), pp. 40 ff.
4. Historically, this is a modern development. See Michael Roberts, "The Military Revolution: 1560-1650,"*Essays in Swedish History* (Minneapolis: University of Minnesota Press, 1967), pp. 195-268.
5. See, e.g., S. P. Huntington, *The Soldier and the State* (Cambridge: Harvard University Press, 1957); J. W. Masland and L. I. Radway, *Soldiers and Scholars* (Princeton, N.J.: Princeton University Press, 1957).
6. R. K. Merton, "Bureaucratic Structure and Personality," in Merton et al., eds., *Reader in Bureaucracy* (Glencoe, Ill.: Free Press, 1952), p. 361.
7. S. L. A. Marshall, *Men against Fire* (New York: William Morrow, 1947), p. 199.
8. Ibid., pp. 94 ff.
9. This generalization applies only to combat units. The organization of services and supplies represents another problem.
10. "I remember thinking during the drive that officers in high authority, Army and even Corps Commanders, should avoid the proximity of the fighting line, and should not dwell in the atmosphere of the back area of a battlefield. . . . No commander can help being influenced by whatever misery or disorder comes within his limited field of vision." Brigadier General E. L. Spears, *Liaison 1914* (New York: Doubleday, 1931), p. 140.
11. Merton, "Bureaucratic Structure," p. 363. Max Weber, *Essays in Sociology,* trans. and ed. H. H. Gerth and C. W. Mills (London: Kegan & Paul, 1948), pp. 233ff.

12. "That is how things happen in war. General Lanrezac contemplates a possible counter-attack and issues orders accordingly. Half the forces concerned never get the order. He changes his mind, and everyone remains as unaware of his new decision as if he were humming a tune in Mars." Spears, *Liaison,* p. 210.

13. "A senior artillery officer ran in, seemingly on the verge of collapse. 'All the guns in the division are lost,' he almost sobbed. Sir Archibald Murray took a step towards him and getting hold of his shoulders shook him roughly. 'To my knowledge you have seven left,' he said sternly." Ibid., p. 284.

14. Marshall, *Men against Fire,* pp. 175 ff.

15. "The flow of men and matériel during battle is ever toward the front. But the prevailing flow of information, on which the employment of men and matériel in combat and the writing of orders and instructions for combat are based, is ever toward the rear, and the volume of it seems to increase according to the square of the distance from the fighting line." Ibid., p. 100.

16. Ibid., pp. 85 ff.

17. Spears, *Liaison,* pp. 76 ff., 323 ff.

18. "The Staff officers . . . formed an aristocracy within the great body of professional officers. Indeed, they seemed to consider themselves the High Priests of the profession, the repositories of the True Faith, the Adepts." Ibid., p. 27. This is a description of the French General Staff. The German General Staff had even greater prestige and authority.

19. Gordon Craig, *The Politics of the Prussian Army* (New York: Oxford University Press, 1956), p. 301. See also G. Ritter, *The Schlieffen Plan* (New York: Praeger, 1958).

20. Marshall, *Men against fire,* pp. 101 ff.

21. Ibid., p. 94.

22. In World War II, for example, the United States Marines were much more inclined to carry out operations regardless of casualties than the more civilian-oriented army.

23. John Terrain, "The Campaign in the Mud," The Spectator, no. 6545 (4 October 1957), pp. 426-427.

24. The Spectator, no. 6757 (27 December 1957); p. 894; no. 6758 (3 January 1958); p. 17; no. 6759 (10 January 1958); p. 47.

25. The adoption of this point of view gave Pétain his great post-World War I reputation. See B. H. Liddell Hart, *The Real War* (Boston: Little, Brown, 1930), pp. 420-425.; P. Valéry, "Réponse au Maréchal Pétain," *Varieté IV* (Paris: Gallimard, 1938), pp. 60 ff.

26. In a strict sense, the above considerations apply only to armies considered as professional bureaucratic organizations. It is both theoretically and practically possible to keep the locus of decision making in the front line; Marshall claims that this has been accomplished in the Israeli army. See S. L. A. Marshall, "Why the Israeli Army Wins," Harper's Magazine 217 (October 1958): 38-45. But the conditions under which this has been accomplished are most pertinent: (1) a citizen rather than a regular army; (2) an egalitarian rather than a hierarchical military status structure; and (3) a military doctrine (and geographical reality) denying the existence of a strategic and logistical rear. How far these conditions are unique to contemporary Israel, how much dependent on the nature of its Arab neighbors, and what possibility there is of applying them to the standing armies of the great powers, are questions of the broadest military and sociological scope. But then, in 1956-1973, the growing professionalization of the Israeli army and the achievement of a strategic and logistical rear area partially nullified these factors.

Chapter 4

THE MILITARY SELF-IMAGE
IN A TECHNOLOGICAL ENVIRONMENT

This chapter explores the implications of technological change for the self-image of the military professional. In addition to developing a set of concepts, it seeks to use the contents of service journals over the past thirty years as an indicator of changing notions of professional identity. I have chosen technology because developments in that area have clearly demonstrable consequences. Technological developments have results that can be observed, tabulated, and analyzed. At the moment a tool, previously unknown or unavailable, comes to be employed, its presence or absence is verifiable in concrete terms. (In 1914, for example, the German army had heavy artillery in significant quantities and the French army did not.) Questions of belief, acceptance, and comprehension are immaterial. In this, technological change differs from changes in organization, ideology, or authority structure.

TYPES OF TECHNOLOGICAL CHANGE

The kinds of technological changes that affect a military system can be ascribed to three general areas. First, there is the kind of innovation that involves instruments which are conventionally and

From **The New Military**, *ed. Morris Janowitz (New York: Russell Sage Foundation, 1964), pp. 159-188. © 1964 Russell Sage Foundation.*

exclusively military in use, such as the submarine snorkel or the recoilless artillery piece. Second, there are those innovations which are adopted in a nonmilitary environment for reasons independent of military considerations but nevertheless have a profound effect on the development and operations of armed forces. The Bessemer process and the canning industry can be cited as examples. Third, there are innovations which are developed in a nonmilitary environment but whose application becomes conspicuously military. The theory of ballistics and the development of nuclear weapons are instances of this kind of innovation. In the interests of brevity, these three categories will be referred to as *arsenal, industrial,* and *laboratory* developments, respectively.

Arsenal Developments

The distinguishing characteristic of arsenal developments is that they represent obviously desirable improvements of conventional instruments. The instruments they modify are already familiar and acceptable to all military men. The research which led to their development could not conceivably have taken place with any other objectives or under any other sponsorship.

Industrial Developments

Industrial developments correspond to a form of change which occurs virtually independent of military needs or objectives. Their acceptance by society is by and large unrelated to their military utility. They are undertaken because they seem theoretically interesting or generally useful. The research which produced them would have taken place had there been no state of warfare or no armed force. Their advantage represents a windfall gained by the organization through its incidental feature of belonging to some society.

Laboratory Developments

Finally, laboratory developments have the distinguishing characteristic of being undertaken for the purpose of a technological revolution. They are, in one way or another, either incomprehensible or unacceptable to the established military professional. Their utility is apparent to the innovator rather than to the consumer; generally they must be imposed on the soldier by some third party. Nevertheless, they are developed with some specific military application in mind. Laboratory research, therefore, is normally sponsored by nonmilitary agencies on the assumption that it represents an approach which the armed forces are inherently incapable of undertaking. Implicit in this is the understanding that the resulting innovation will be resisted by the official agencies and that some extraordinary pressure may be necessary for its adoption. In the contemporary transformation of the military establishment, the armed forces are seeking to overcome their resistance to technological change. Thus the military itself may support and sponsor laboratory developments.

Both the arsenal and the industrial concepts represent relatively manageable modes of innovation, as the required process of adjustment does not of itself involve any radical changes in the structure of military organization. In arsenal developments, the novelties are both foreseen and desired. Moreover, since the process of development is entirely under military control, the acceptance or rejection of specific ideas is generally routine procedure. In industrial developments, the innovations take place independently of military considerations. Their acceptance or rejection, therefore, is arbitrary and fortuitous. Neither of these lines of technological research forsees any application outside of the social and institutional setting which has sponsored it. Neither is normally subject to pressures and procedures over which the parent body has no control.

Laboratory developments, on the other hand, in order to be effective, must gain the support of individuals other than those actually involved in the process of inaugurating and carrying them out. They begin as the exclusive concern of strictly nonmilitary persons, but if this development process is to be ultimately successful, it must be actively advanced by influential members of some armed force and its particular techniques must be actively incorporated into the official body of standard institutional expertise.

There is a value in contrasting this situation with what has been designated as industrial development. While improvements in the techniques of metallurgy and food preservation are of obvious interest to the armed forces and may even be sponsored by them, there is no conventionally pressing need to incorporate the techniques involved in such advances into the accepted image of a professionally competent officer. If the capacity for such improvements is recognized in the society with which the armed force is affiliated, the military may subsidize research and set up agencies to inspire a more effective military utilization of results. But fundamentally the military will agree that this process is essentially a civilian concern which would take place in any case short of coercive prohibition, and perhaps even then. The end product is designed for a civilian market and is subject to its demands. Its military utility is incidental.

However, the evolution of ballistic theory and the development of nuclear weapons were undertaken with specific military applications in mind. Each experiment could have been a success yet the project a failure, purely on the basis of its rejection by the institution to which it was offered. The failure would not have resided in the specialized activity of the developers but in their incidental efforts to convert members of the military establishment to their point of view. From this it may be inferred that the emphasis of laboratory specialists is not primarily on the transformation of their own techniques but on the modification and even subversion of the traditional self-sufficiency of the professional military image. The discoveries of the laboratory specialist are designed to demonstrate that the existing expertise in the military body represents a haphazard and inadequate approach to the problems with which it must deal.

Arsenal developments, finally, are completely under military control, from authorization to acceptance or rejection. An armed force may pay the penalty of defeat for refusing to adopt an improvement within its grasp—for retaining a muzzle-loading musket, for example, when breech-loading rifles are available. But the decision is entirely its own. Within the context of its society, there is no other potential customer and no other body of experts to dispute the propriety of its choice.

Officer Image and Technological Change

These three approaches imply a particular kind of relationship of individuals to the armed forces they serve. Officers involved in the process of technological change may be regarded as innovators, deviants, or marginal men. These descriptive terms imply not only that the organization is being served in a particular way but also that the manner of service is related to the organization's self-image and to the relationship which it believes exists between it and society.

The individuals responsible for arsenal developments have already been accepted as part of the military establishment. The fate of their particular product does not prima facie affect their position in the military. The adoption or rejection of proposals may, of course, determine short-term success or failure in a chosen career, but the individuals are assured of a post. In joining the arsenal, the military technician accedes to the institutional decision-making process and is presumably resigned to the inherent risks. Loyalty to the organization is considered to be stronger than devotion to research. The arsenal concept accordingly permits an armed force to allow some of its members to be *innovators* without running the risk that they may become *deviants*.

Industrial developments, however, are undertaken by individuals who have neither the desire to apply nor the attributes of being acceptable to the organization. They are members of a class which is by definition nonmilitary; their skills, even when accepted at their highest evaluation, will never be included within the official definition of professional military expertise. A career soldier who specializes in such procedures will invariably be a *deviant,* although at times a useful one. He may perform a valuable service in bringing remote, though pertinent, information to the attention of the proper authorities. But insofar as his interests centered on such matters, his professional capacities and his career prospects would be regarded as impaired, and he himself would be regarded as the kind of example to be discouraged.

The protagonists of laboratory developments, for their part, occupy the position of *marginal* men. They represent individuals who have undertaken to make their characteristic talents essential to the armed force without in any real sense applying for admission to it. The decision to accept such skills as being either deviant or innovative is one which the armed force has to make according to its conception of the specific merits of each case. Every laboratory development claims to be simultaneously a radical improvement of military techniques and an outright subverter of established military traditions. A professional officer, in identifying himself with programs of this kind, makes a critical decision. If he is successful in getting the novelty accepted as essential to the proper performance of military missions, his career prospects are greatly enhanced. If he fails, he suffers the penalty for having openly aided influences which have been officially recognized and rejected as hostile to the established order.

In applying these concepts to the military, we may say in formal terms that we are dealing with two contrasting models of organizational outlook. One, like the guardian class in Plato's *Republic,* views itself as the sole and exclusive elite agency in its society, the only body capable of rational behavior. The other is committed to a pluralistic vision of society and accordingly views itself as one among many collaborating bodies of rationally motivated experts. The first type will be referred to henceforth as *primitive,* the second as *competitive.*

Primitive military organizations characteristically consider themselves to be the embodiment of rational practices. They select as leaders only the genuinely rational and superior applicants. Rejected candidates and nonapplicants are thus inferior to members of the organization.

At any given moment, therefore, a primitive organization represents the fullest possible realization of its potential strength.

Insofar as numbers and knowledge are concerned, it has nothing to gain from any further dealings with the outside world. Since the organization, moreover, is the embodiment of rationality, there is no higher form of existence than official behavior. All members of the military, by the fact of their membership, possess these superior qualities. The total absorption of all its members in the institutional routine is, therefore, a rational objective. The round of drills, rituals, and disciplinary measures results in a range of refined characteristics according to which every member can identify himself with the organization and by which his identification will be recognized by every other member.

By definition, therefore, a primitive armed force confines its activities to the body of its actual members. The organization regards itself as embodying the state of nature, and the outside world as representing the possibility of corruption and the fall of man. Consequently, insofar as the organization has the power, certain characteristics or virtues considered desirable become, also by definition, a natural military monopoly. This includes not only the military virtues but also any factor which could affect the existence of the armed force as a self-sufficient monopoly. Thus, for example, landownership, literacy, and the right of assembly have in the past been claimed as the exclusive privileges of military leaders who embody the primitive outlook. Such privileges do not necessarily increase military efficiency, but their preemption by members of the military makes it difficult for nonmembers to achieve an independent bargaining position.

The primitivist approach systematically includes an image of the outside world which is essentially negative in nature. It describes and regulates its external environment in terms of the absence of those very traits which it believes to be essential for the maintenance of a coherent social scheme. Nonmembership, inferiority, and disorganization are equivalent terms.

The competitive approach, on the other hand, holds that no single profession or organization has a monopoly of effective rational behavior. Society, insofar as it leads to interaction among its members, develops distinctive bodies of operational criteria and systematic rules, and it is on the basis of skill and mastery in such areas, rather than on the simple fact of membership in one social group or another, that the attribution of rationality is determined. Thus there are rational and nonrational soldiers, just as there are rational and nonrational members of other professions. Rationality refers to occupational proficiency rather than social affiliation.

Thus, a competitively oriented organization has few built-in inhibitions about recognizing the existence of rational individuals who do not belong to it. And, as a rationally oriented body, it is prepared to admit the existence of some individuals in the outside world who are, according to its own definitions, acceptable as members or active collaborators. If such individuals are civilians, it is either because, at a given moment, the organization has no need for their services, or because it is unable to provide them with sufficient inducement to join it.

With such assumptions, it is impossible for a competitively oriented organization to assume attainment of the optimum level of efficiency, except perhaps in a purely military sense. But it is not easy to give a precise definition to the term "purely military." Indeed, given the assumption of the existence of a plurality of rational groups, an armed force has no "purely military" method for determining whether or not it is taking full advantage of the available range of rational skills. Characteristic expertise relates only to its own operations, and every other system of rational procedures is equally self-sufficient. Unless members of other professions can be persuaded to make their knowledge available to the competitively oriented armed force, it is in no position to evaluate the potential utility of such contributions.

Active collaboration rather than isolated self-sufficiency is, therefore, the guiding objective of a competitively oriented organization. To the extent that they are able to cooperate with other groups of experts, competitively oriented experts achieve an adequate degree of understanding of the outside world.

Now it can be objected that, as formal organizations, armed forces are unique and therefore lack criteria for measuring the achievements of nonmilitary groups. In a primitively oriented sense this statement is perhaps true. But it can be argued that, once it has accepted the competitive principle, an armed force becomes increasingly more heterogeneous and similar in form and composition to the society supporting it, and that the cumulative result of competitive orientation is an accelerating tendency toward the expansion and diversification of the elite group. The greater the range of skills encompassed by its activities, the better its ability to appreciate the potential contribution of outside groups.

Primitive and competitive orientations accordingly carry with them their own particular adaptation to technological change. A strict *arsenal* approach to development activities is the necessary condition of primitive military control. The kinds of changes which may directly affect military techniques are explored under the exclusive sponsorship of the armed forces. Research outside military control is considered to have little or no direct bearing on the problems of the military profession. There is no forseeable reason for the organization to adjust its internal structure to changes taking place in the outside world.

An armed force which, on the other hand, is prepared to respond consciously to external developments in techniques is an expression of the competitive model, although in this respect it can be either passive or active. As a passive agency it would adopt the *industrial* approach, not collaborating directly in the rational pursuits of nonmilitary professionals but also not suffering from any inhibitions in taking advantage of them. The industrial approach is characteristic of a period of organizational transition during which the primitive approach is recognized as untenable but the competitive orientation has not yet been fully accepted. As an active competitive agency, the military would adopt the *laboratory* approach and officially sponsor the research and development processes to modify its own proper professional standards. Military efficiency would be equated with the inclusion of the greatest possible range of nonmilitary skills within the context of the organization, and active leaders of the armed force be eager to demonstrate their receptivity to technological change.

Many areas of critical technological change will harbor a conflict between proponents of the arsenal type of development and proponents of the laboratory approach. The attitude of a particular armed force toward these protagonists will be determined by the image it has of itself as either a primitive or a competitively oriented body. As the former, it will admit as innovations only those techniques developed in its own arsenals; it will treat as deviants the proponents of any type of externally developed change. This does not mean that change from without will be unacceptable but, rather, that the proponents of such change may be penalized in their career prospects even when successful in their advocacy. A competitively oriented organization, on the other hand, will seek to balance the developments of independent experts with its own internally generated process of change. It will institute programs to encourage the widest possible range of outside professional contacts among its personnel.

PRIMITIVE VERSUS COMPETITIVE MILITARY ORGANIZATION

The five basic hypotheses of *The Professional Soldier,* by Morris Janowitz, can be examined in the light of these contentions and translated into these concepts of primitive versus competitive military organization. The combination will, I believe, indicate possible lines of empirical investigation into the operation of military organizations.

Changing Organizational Authority

The shift from domination to manipulation and persuasion entails a transformation in the organization's self-image—from that of an autonomous homogeneous body to that of a holding company, exploiting the most rewarding combination of enterprises attainable. Under the primitive approach, a strictly prescribed mode of development was in force; the organization maintained rigid criteria for the kinds of innovation it was willing to accept. Change in general, particularly unforseen change, was considered undesirable. The process of modification would therefore be entrusted exclusively to individuals satisfying the organization's standards of indoctrination and control; no improvement would be acceptable unless it gave the appearance of having been officially anticipated. The individual skills involved would be considered characteristically military in a manner satisfying the force's contention that it was the sole valid judge of the meaning of the results. It is symptomatic of the primitive-arsenal approach that developments with obvious military applicability are rejected on the grounds that they are detrimental to the spirit which unifies and inspires the armed force. A list of prominent examples, ranging from firearms to the guided missile, documents this response. The attitude inherent in this reaction is that the cohesion and effectiveness of an armed force rest on an orthodoxy of practice and belief. The techniques and the ideals of the profession are presented as a single immutable whole.

Competitive-laboratory developments, in contrast, represent breakthroughs into areas previously unfamiliar to the professional soldier. This fact in itself prevents the organization from using its own criteria to assess the changes involved. The experts under consideration would have to be treated as autonomous agents obtaining special benefits in return for making their services freely available. The relationship between a given armed force and its specialists would be of mutual advantage, and the atypical nature of experts would be overtly recognized in the formal relations between them and members of the organization. Instead of rigid discipline, inducements such as civic honors, notably high salaries, and appeals to patriotism would be employed to achieve the desired results. Indeed, it would be an article of faith, subscribed to by both parties, that rigid compulsion frustrates development.

Narrowing Skill Differential between Military and Civilian Elites

The primitivist approach implies a sharp either/or distinction between arsenal and other modes of development, so that the possibility of confusion between innovators and deviants is, for all practical purposes, eliminated. Only that research which is officially sponsored and internally staffed can yield acceptable results.

There is, inherent in the arsenal approach, a tendency to accept only anticipated consequences; by this mechanism the organization's self-image of a self-sufficient monopoly is maintained. The skills it does not command are therefore by definition antithetical to the ideals of the primitive armed force. The unauthorized innovator is almost invariably treated as a deviant.

The competitive approach, by contrast, systematically seeks out those very skills it perceives to be absent in its table of organization. An obviously efficacious industrial or scientific technique represents a challenge to systematic military development. Recognized nonmilitary experts are viewed as promising "crash programs" and "breakthroughs" which will radically extend the state of military art. The professional value of the soldier increases to the extent that he is sensitive to the possibilities of technical improvement inherent in the surrounding society. There is, therefore, a career premium attached to a demonstrated familiarity with the prevalent range of civilian expertise, and a tacit assurance that personal commitment to any established nonmilitary specialty will result in the career rewards of innovation rather than in the penalties of deviancy. The laboratory model includes in this innovation concepts and data based on the social sciences.

The Shift in Officer Recruitment

The sharp contrast between military and nonmilitary behavior inherent in the primitive approach leads the organization toward the recruitment ideal of a self-sustaining caste. The dominant personnel preoccupation is that of preserving the system from contamination by the nonmilitary world. Soldiers are therefore sought from those classes which seem least likely to be influenced by forces of social change over which the armed forces exercise no direct control. In reciprocal fashion, those elements of society with the least contact and sympathy with the general process of social change turn to the armed forces as promising an environment in which their traditional values will be cherished and protected from the threat of obsolescence.

A general and naive suspicion of unanticipated change provides a common ground. Under the primitive model, the military seem to operate on the assumption that the narrower the social base of officer recruitment, the greater the certainty of enforcing a standard pattern for the belief and behavior of the individuals involved. The maintenance of a rigid orthodoxy becomes progressively more difficult as the number of active personnel increase. The officer caste is therefore drawn from a self-conscious and deliberate minority group. In such a system, deviancy is relatively simple both to recognize and to define. The determined deviant individual, moreover, has no motivation for undertaking the strenuous and risky effort of entering and persisting in a military career.

Under the competitive approach, however, the efficiency of the organization is assumed to increase with the widening of the range of encompassed skills. Armed forces are therefore encouraged to operate on the broadest possible recruiting base, and individuals are given reason to believe that those with esoteric attitudes, backgrounds, and skills will have real prospects offered to them by a military career. Military organizations come to be regarded as especially representative institutions, open and receptive to a wide variety of talent.

Significance of Career Patterns

The primitive approach is characterized by the belief that the military profession represents a unique and exclusive way of life, one which is diametrically opposed to the habits and customs of the outside world. As such, it is an ideal to be pursued by military members. Within this context, therefore, there is a hierarchy of career patterns, ranked according to the degree in which they are considered to permit the realization of pure military conduct. Cavalry officers have been, for example, traditionally considered to be more military than artillerymen or engineers; the latter suffer from a dependence on techniques and instruments developed and employed in the nonmilitary world. As a practical matter, advancement prospects are directly allocated on the basis of the degree of "purity" attached to a given military assignment, and the scale is so clearly defined that every officer knows fairly well what to expect. This has the consequence, either deliberate or unconscious, of enforcing custom. Officers realize that a branch of service is evaluated according to its demonstrated adherence to tradition. Traditional branches clearly offer the best prospects for promotion. The best connected and most typical recruits are accordingly the ones who gain admission to these branches. Marginal types can hope only for commissions in unorthodox services. Moreover, since the inner elite is by and large made up of members of the traditional branches, official policy favors their outlook and techniques.

In a competitive system, on the other hand, no such hierarchy can exist. The contribution of each branch is measured, not in pure military terms, but according to the estimate of the range and fruitfulness of general techniques that it is able to encompass. Entrance to the inner elite is to a large part determined by a demonstrated breadth of contacts and sympathies with prominent members of the nonmilitary world. Under these circumstances, accordingly, the least traditional branches can compete, if only because their members are likely to have fewer inhibitions in adapting to emerging military problems. In any event, there is no pure military type to serve as a hierarchic model, except perhaps the rather contradictory ideal of a dedicated and loyal soldier who can, when necessary, free himself from all considerations of established military tradition and standard military procedure.

Trends in Political Indoctrination

Honor and tradition are the reigning standards of the primitive approach. An armed force of this kind tends to regard itself as a self-sufficient body. Its corporate behavior is designed to reinforce and maintain its own idiosyncratic code. Legitimate political objectives correspond to the social and economic conditions represented by the official military privileges and responsibilities. The officer who satisfies organizational standards satisfies all the criteria of political orthodoxy. A soldier whose background and behavior are in some degree atypical is a probable subversive. In one sense, then, a primitivist officer can be described as apolitical;

so long as the established pattern of his own organization is unaffected, he is likely to have no interest in the competition for status and power taking place in the outside world. On the other hand, he can be regarded as intensely politically oriented, in that he may consider any nonmilitary intervention in military policy as a threat both to his society and to his existence and therefore as a justification for an open and all-out military attack on the interfering agencies. The values he is committed to are those of his organization, and in that cause there are no inhibitions about the kind and degree of intervention he is prepared to practice in the nonmilitary world.

Members of a competitive organization, by contrast, accept the legitimacy of the application of nonmilitary standards to the conduct of military operations. This is not merely because it is assumed that military acts have political and social consequences, and that to a significant extent the organization is responsible for these consequences. It also stems from a prudent desire to hedge bets. Professional competence, according to the competitive approach, is directly related to awareness of professional limitations. The rational outlook is a product of conscious specialization and depends on interaction with authorities from diverse fields. The participation of nonmilitary experts in the formulation of military plans provides an assurance, not only that a number of rational approaches will be put to work on the particular problem, but also that the necessary specialization of individual experts will be neutralized by the unrestricted collaboration of a multiplicity of independent minds.

But active collaboration is also an essential ingredient of professional self-esteem. In a competitively oriented environment, general utility rather than parochial self-sufficiency is the dominant criterion. The specialist in one particular field needs, in order to achieve his full professional stature, some form of assurance that his behavior has been found rational by the general community of experts and that the manner in which he pursues his profession gives the greatest possible degree of encouragement and stimulus to theirs.

Membership in this community of experts entails adherence to its own special etiquette. Each participant is expected to understand and restrict himself to his particular role. According to the logic of military technological development, the competitively oriented officer is a consumer as well as a producer of results. If nonmilitary skills are to improve and extend the range of military operations, those who use them must be free to develop according to their own inner criteria. The organization encourages disinterested researchers and adapts their results to the solution of its particular problems. It agrees with the general assumption that to impose its own particular outlook on the course of investigation would be to deprive itself of the resources of objective science. On the political and technical levels, the competitively oriented officer seeks the kind of relationship that enables him to understand the problems of nonmilitary techniques and to collaborate sympathetically in underwriting and applying their discoveries.

Do these considerations illuminate the tensions presently operating within the American military establishment? The establishment's awareness of the tremendous technological resources of modern society presents it with multiple alternative courses of development with respect to not only the instruments it employs but also the forms of organization adopted. Every step in the direction of increased efficiency entangles the armed force in a complex of attendant problems arising from the fact that new skills may be thereby required or that established professional standards may be thereby rendered obsolete. The organization is confronted with a conflict of values. It can take the fullest possible advantage of the technological resources of its society and relegate the maintenance of its own characteristic professional standards and identity to secondary importance. Or it can claim that its major role is to produce professional soldiers with characteristic military skills which have the fullest possible scope for rational application. Then the professionals can refuse or modify techniques or instruments that may radically modify the organizational climate.

The result of such choices can be analyzed from two directions: what the armed forces feel they are expected to be, and what they would like to be—namely, the self-image of the professional. When, as in a primitively oriented body, the two coincide, the problem is not too serious. When, as in a competitively oriented force, the professional soldier feels that he is expected to be a member of a body of rationally oriented experts recognized as such by the general professional community, the problem becomes more complicated. For the general community of the professionally educated, little value is placed on the intense form of parochial allegiance which appears to be so essential to military life. The civilian concept of military professionalism is likely to be drawn on the model of scientific objectivity and moral neutrality, while the military ideal of a professional soldier tends to include the assumption of a deep commitment to certain moral and group values.

The argument is reduced to the contention that, to the degree that an armed force remains primitive, it loses its efficiency, and to the degree that it becomes competitive, it loses its identity. The fact that both primitive and competitive orientations can adapt themselves to technology—the one in the arsenal form, the other, in the laboratory—does not affect the situation. Their characteristic limitations are transferred to new fields. The result in reality is a personal and organizational effort to fuse orientations and create a viable balance.

The course of contemporary military technology provides some evidence for this contention. The assignment of specific areas of research and development to particular branches of service has frequently resulted in the elevation of the instruments involved into a kind of ultimate value. Primitive values are wedded to the most familiar machine. The retention of a particular kind of weapons system becomes an end in itself. The primitive organization treats as inconceivable the claim that its distinctive mission could be better carried out, or even carried out in any form, by any other instrument. To the extent that technological expertise is defined as part of the professional role, the relevant skills and practices are ritually associated with the instrument around which they originally evolved. If, on the other hand, the laboratory approach is adopted, and research and development are entrusted to purely scientific and technological bodies, the armed forces may be regarded as lacking in the expertise necessary for responsible control. The control of intercontinental missiles is a crucial case in point. Military experience provides only a partial basis for asserting a special understanding of such instruments. The individual military officer can be inducted into the weapons system after assimilating himself to the class of experts that originally developed it. But to control even the missile requires more than technical expertise; it requires a military posture to guarantee local security and to ensure compliance with strategic commands.

Perhaps the differences are essentially related to the concept of control. From the primitive point of view, it is the military organization that must be controlled. That condition realized, the environment presents no problems. From the competitive point of view, however, various organizations merely represent alternative devices for controlling the general environment. Diplomacy, economic policy, or even education, for example, may be considered to be just as effective as military action for attaining a desirable international order.

ROLE OF SERVICE JOURNALS

There are a variety of empirical approaches to studying long-term shifts in professional self-images, from primitivist to competitive. If one wants to employ quantitative data, service journals, studied by systematic content analysis, supply indicators of changing self-conceptions and of efforts to fuse the component elements. For this purpose, two journals were reviewed during the period 1936-1959. For the navy, the sponsored journal was the *U.S. Naval Institute Proceedings;* for the army, it was the *Infantry Journal—Combat Forces—Army,* the three titles through which the ground force publication evolved. This sample has the double advantage of covering the period of professional transformation and of selecting for intensive study years when there were no overt military hostilities.

In terms of the interaction of role concept and professional ideology occurring in the officer corps of the United States armed forces somewhere between 1936-1959, the basic hypotheses of this chapter are explicit. In the post-World War II period, the prevalent ideology of the armed forces, as manifested in their professional journals, contained strong elements of a primitive orientation. The post-World War II era has witnessed an intensified development of the competitive outlook with its managerial professional ideology. Before World War II, the emphasis was on the stability of the military environment and the maintenance of institutional efficiency through the conscientious performance of routine assignments. The conceived role of the armed forces was not so much that of adjusting to changes in the outside world as of continually perfecting themselves in executing their natural military functions.

Since World War II, the armed forces have been increasingly involved in the continual process of adjusting to the manifold changes—technological, economic, political, and sociological—in the world which surrounds them. Professional discourse centers not so much on the perfection of performance in routine assignments as on the anticipation of significant changes in the world arena and on the formulation of necessary decisions.

According to these hypotheses, the service journal would reflect any shifts in the concerns of the officer corps of the United States. In the framework of this analysis the service journal may be said to have become more professional in the intervening period; that is to say, more rational in the bureaucratic and organizational sense. The possible range of military events has become increasingly complex. Armed forces were at one time expected to be prepared for at most two or three kinds of war. Now they are expected to maintain a capability for all responsibilities between arms-control enforcement and total war. But this is only partially true. Before World War II, the navy had already changed its self-concept by weakening its primitivist military component and incorporating important elements of the competitive outlook.

At this point it is appropriate to advance some observations about the institutional role played by service journals. Sponsored periodicals are by no means an exclusive feature of the armed forces. Almost every professional body maintains something of that nature as part of its organizational apparatus and generally as a component of its educational activities.

To operate effectively, organized professionals generally maintain an apparatus for recruiting and training members. They also support at least one publication for the dissemination of common ideas and experiences. Every organized profession, in short, has its seminary, academy, or graduate school—and its journal.

The organization of professional education is much older and seems much more natural than the professional practice of sponsoring a periodical. The existence of an educational organization staffed and administered by senior members provides a profession with a means both of determining the acceptability of applicants and of instilling in them critical standards, essential factual background, and a sense of professional cohesion.

The reason for the existence of professional journals seems less striking. Why should the professional be expected to contribute articles to professional journals? And why should his writings be published in a medium supervised by the profession of which he is a member? There is an obvious difference between the two institutions: graduation from the proper school automatically confers professional status; publication of one's writings does not.

Doctors, lawyers, soldiers, scientists, and members of other organized or regulated professions do in general write for one another. When they write as professionals, their work is submitted to journals sponsored by the profession and edited or supervised by senior members. In writing for publication, therefore, members of the regulated professions are subjecting themselves to yet another form of organized control.

From this point of view, publication can be regarded as a postgraduate form of professional policing. It enables the organization to appraise and reward the activities of mature members. Efforts which conform to established standards and which deal with subjects of professional significance are guaranteed an appreciative audience. The professional who has works published is authoritatively presented as a person whose activities and thoughts merit the serious attention of his peers. The military, like any other highly trained, rationally oriented professional body, realizes the value of disseminating rapidly and in a universal manner significant developments in techniques and doctrines. It needs some vehicle for emphasizing significant issues.

But there is one respect in which soldiers do differ from other professionals. The United States military establishment is a more comprehensive institution. Doctors, lawyers, and many other professionals are not encompassed by an institutional structure which takes upon itself the task not only of assigning to each member a particular role but also of furnishing him with the equipment and information considered necessary to his position. With regard to information, at least, most professionals are relatively free and independent performers. In both giving and receiving information, they have wide latitude in setting their own standards and practices. Professional soldiers, however, operate within a structure which not only defines official behavior but also provides a copious and detailed flow of printed instructions on how they are to perform. It also uses a set of checks and procedures to ensure that official literature is read by its designated audience.

If the military organization furnishes its members with the details and doctrines pertinent to their particular assignments, what justification is there for a professional journal? The existence and promulgation of official doctrine do not necessarily imply that there is no room for further discussion. But since the journals themselves are officially sanctioned, a question arises about the role such discussion is assumed to play. For both the United States Army and the United States Navy, as concrete examples, there are two distinct bodies of printed literature edited and written predominantly by members of the profession: (1) manuals and directives assigned to every active member on the basis of his particular assignment (assigned literature); and (2) journals made available to every interested party, active or inactive, professional or layman, on a general and unregulated basis (sponsored literature).

The examination of assigned literature is beyond the scope of this paper. In many respects, however, the function of assigned literature is clear. It is an instrument of efficiency and control, a sort of impersonal and complex command. In short, it tells the officers what they need to know.

THE MEANING OF SPONSORED LITERATURE

Sponsored literature obviously must also respond to a need of the organization. Particular articles in a sponsored channel can, at best, be justified by the fact that they tell soldiers what they may want to know. The sponsored journal, it is assumed, reaches areas of professional interest inaccessible to official publications. But this assumption does not provide us with clear-cut criteria for assessing the significance of or reason for printing particular articles. If the information contained is considered vital to organizational effectiveness, why was it not circulated through official channels? If the information presented is of peripheral interest, why, in an organization devoted to discipline and decisiveness, publish it at all?

Sponsored literature, unlike the body of assigned literature, is an area of voluntary contributions. This does not mean that some contributors may not have been invited to submit articles but that, if invited, they generally were in a position to decline. A journal made up entirely of command performances would be a specimen of assigned literature. Sponsored literature provides the soldier with the opportunity to display his ability and to impress his superiors on subjects and under circumstances which are, in general, his own choice. His choice must, of course, conform in some essential respect to that of established authority and practice. But the soldier who has articles published operates to some extent outside regular channels. He not only provides ideas and information to his peers; he also—and especially in the lower grades—provides them with a model of a certain kind of professional autonomy as well as competence.

The military profession therefore sponsors and maintains a considerable number of professional journals designed for an audience of professional soldiers. All three services of the United States armed forces, for example, have their official or quasi-official publications, and many of the subordinate branches also have journals of their own. Contributions are solicited from active duty officers. Like all other professional journals, the published contents of the service journals are expected by the editors to express personal and presumably original points of view.

Editorial content in a service journal is not a form of command. A published article may be disregarded. However, professionals are expected to read their journals, not in order to be told what to do, but rather to be informed about what it is important to think about. Thus, for the purposes of this analysis of professional self-image, it is especially important to study sponsored literature. The prevalent military self-image is that of a man of action, yet the concept of professionalization entails a notion of rational behavior. The complete soldier, therefore, is an individual who under appropriate circumstances does what he is told, without hesitation, and at other times carefully examines the situation before deciding upon a course of action.

TRENDS IN CONTENT OF SERVICE JOURNALS

Two journals, *Infantry Journal—Combat Forces—Army*, and *U.S. Naval Institute Proceedings,* were analyzed for 1936-1938, 1947-1949, and 1957-1959. (Because of its comparatively recent origin, the U.S. Air Force had no sponsored publication for the first two periods.) Both journals have a quasi-official status. Each is sponsored, supervised, and edited by representatives of the services it professes to serve. Final responsibility and control have always been in the hands of a senior retired officer. Editorial standards can, therefore, be presumed to conform to the professional standards and objectives of the organization. This does not mean that published articles were intended to be accepted as official statements of doctrine. But the presumption does exist that printed material was viewed as indicative of the beliefs, interests, and problems considered useful and proper for the various ranks.

The first measure of trends in content was the relative distribution of articles by military and by civilian writers. Crude though this measure may be, it can be taken as an indicator of the relative emphasis on a primitive versus a competitive orientation. The extent to which a journal revealed an exclusive reliance on military authors would be a measure of organization exclusiveness (primitive outlook) and a resistance to competitive relations with civilian society.

The trend comparison between the army- and the navy-sponsored publications on this measure is most revealing. As in so many other content categories, the navy revealed a remarkable stability throughout the three periods from 1936 through 1959; roughly 75 per cent of the articles in each period were written by military personnel (table 1). Moreover, in comparison with the army, the navy establishment's technological base clearly produced an earlier incorporation of civilian figures and a trend away from the primitive model. The army journal in 1936-1938 was decidedly more exclusive; over 90 per cent of its articles were written by the military. The army trend is one of wide fluctuation, reaching a low point in 1947-1949, when military contributors dropped to two-thirds and civilian contributors reached one-third, a figure in excess of that for the navy. The short-term change was a response to new politico-military conditions with an exaggerated shift toward the competitive model even beyond that of the navy. The search for a new equilibrium can be seen by the fact that, by 1957-1959, the period of maximum retrenchment, civilian contributions to the army journal declined sharply to 16 per cent. The "primitivist" component was strengthened temporarily. While these civilian contributions were not so low as before World War II, they were decidedly lower than in the navy. Thus, the army evolved a more competitive approach but still remained more primitively oriented than the navy.

The second content trend in the service journals relevant for professional identity concerned the type of subject matter contained in these publications. A simple classification into broad professional, narrow professional or technical, and human interest articles is relevant for this type of analysis. *Broad professional* refers to articles of apparent interest to all officers, such as historical accounts, for example, errors of the Korean conflict; morale building (the objectives of leadership); mission defining (the role of the navy in the Cold War); applied strategy (controlled retaliation). *Narrow professional* or technical refers to specific tactical and technical problems of direct interest to particular groups of specialists, for example, antitank mine simulation. Human interest articles are addressed to the military not as soldiers but as members of a certain socioeconomic group; for example, articles might describe fishing in Alaska, investing for retirement, etc.

Table 1: Army- and Navy-Sponsored Literature, 1936-1959: Distribution of Military and Civilian Authors

Distribution of Articles	1936-1938	1947-1949	1957-1959	Total
	(Percentages)			
Army				
Military Contributors	91	66	84	
Civilian Contributors	9	34	16	
Total	100	100	100	
Number of articles	224	267	291	782
Navy				
Military Contributors	76	77	74	
Civilian Contributors	24	23	26	
Total	100	100	100	
Number of articles	397	351	324	1,072

Table 2: Army- and Navy-Sponsored Literature, 1936-1959: Distribution of Types of Content

Types of Content	1936-1938	1947-1949	1952-1959
	(Percentages)		
Army			
Broad Professional	68	85	80
Narrow Professional	28	7	16
Human Interest	4	7	3
Total	100	100	100
Navy			
Broad Professional	67	83	83
Narrow Professional	24	15	14
Human Interest	9	2	2
Total	100	100	100
	Breakdown of Broad Professional Articles		
Army			
Historical	29	28	12
Morale Building	14	15	15
Mission Defining	–	9	10
Applied Strategy	25	33	43
Total	68	85	80
Navy			
Historical	37	44	27
Morale Building	14	13	12
Mission Defining	8	11	9
Applied Strategy	8	15	35
Total	67	83	83

Both the army and the navy organs reveal a similar trend, during the period, of increased emphasis on broad professional content and a decline in narrow professional and human interest material (table 2). The concentration of broad professional articles rose, for the army, from 68 to 80 per cent, and from 67 to 83 per cent for the navy. Narrow technical communications declined and their authors found outlets in the more specialized journals, reflecting the increased division of labor in the military. Human interest material became practically nonexistent. The format that emerged is one more compatible with a managerially oriented profession.

These categories highlight again the greater stability of naval institutions. The evolution toward broader professional perspectives was gradual and steady in the naval publication. The army-sponsored publication showed greater fluctuations for the 1947-1949 civilianization period, when narrow professional articles dropped very sharply to only 7 per cent of the content but rose again to 16 per cent in 1957-1959, to a level comparable to the navy.

If the total category of broad professional articles is further subdivided into four component groups—*(a)* historical; *(b)* morale building; *(c)* mission defining; and *(d)* applied strategy (table 2)—the pattern of stability and change emerges more clearly. These categories further highlight the shift from a primitive orientation to a competitive model. Historical material, as presented in these journals, is more an expression of organizational solidarity and fundamental virtues than problem solving. Thus, in both services the sponsored journals showed a decrease in concern with historical presentations; in the army, from 29 to 12 per cent; and in the navy, from 37 to 27 per cent. On the other hand, both journals show an increased concern with applied strategy, to a point where this emerged as the dominant category in 1957-1959, with 43 per cent for the army and 35 per cent for the navy. Applied strategy is an expression of the competitive model to the extent that it is involved in relating military strategy to technological and political developments.

In addition, these broad professional articles help to probe the extent to which each service has been able to develop a fusion between the primitivist and the competitive orientations. It should be noted that in both journals the concentration of morale-building articles—a concern with fundamental group values—has been about equal and has remained persistent. Moreover, the concern with history as a reflection of primitivist values remains at a higher level in the navy journal than in that of the army. Although the navy initiated efforts toward a competitive model earlier, the 1957-1959 period reveals a clear-cut persistence of a core of interest in traditional concerns. The army, in contrast, began the process of adaptation later and in the course fluctuated to a greater extent.

The third measure in content trends analyzed the rank of the contributors during the period under investigation. (For purposes of comparison, in table 3 the breakdowns by rank are presented for all military contributors). A number of observations can be made about these data if the ranks are broken down into four categories: enlisted men; company-grade officers (lieutenant-captain; ensign-lieutenant); field-grade officers (major-colonel; lieutenant commander-captain); and general officers or admirals. (a) As in the other content measures, there is much greater stability of rank levels in the sponsored literature of the navy than of the army, reflecting actual stability in the rank distribution as well as organizational conceptions about rank relations. (b) It was to be expected that the bulk of the writing was done by the middle-level ranks. In both services the field-grade officer is the most frequently represented. The percentage of field-grade officers who are the backbone of the contributors remains relatively stable. For the navy, it rose gradually during the period as a whole (51 to 68 per cent of military contributors). For the army, there is a marked fluctuation for the period immediately after World War II, but stability for the overall period. (c) Enlisted personnel are represented in both organs. For the navy, they have a stable token representation of around 2 or 3 per cent, which reflects the navy's recognition of the existence and accepted position of the enlisted men; while in the army, the percentage has risen from token representation before the war to almost 10 per cent, a reflection of the increased concern with the position of the enlisted man in the ground forces. (d) The great variation that has taken place is the decline of company-grade officers in both services, reflecting

Table 3: Army- and Navy-Sponsored Literature, 1936-1959:
          Rank Distribution of Contributors

Service	1936-1938	1947-1949	1957-1959
	Military and Civilian Contributors (Percentages)		
Army			
Enlisted	2	3	7
Lieutenant-Captain	35	4	14
Major-Colonel	48	47	46
General	6	12	17
Civilian	9	34	16
Total	100	100	100
Navy			
Enlisted	2	3	2
Ensign-Lieutenant	29	13	14
Lt. Commander-Captain	41	54	51
Admiral	4	7	7
Civilian	25	23	26
Total	100	100	100
	Military Contributors Only		
Army			
Enlisted	2	5	8
Lieutenant-Captain	38	6	17
Major-Colonel	53	71	55
General Officer	7	18	20
Total	100	100	100
Navy			
Enlisted	3	4	3
Ensign-Lieutenant	39	17	19
Lt. Commander-Captain	51	70	69
Admiral	7	9	9
Total	100	100	100

the broadening professional conceptions of the journals as well as
the crisis of the position of the junior officer. In the army, the
decline is much sharper and much more subject to fluctuation.
(e) One would have expected an increase in representation of
generals and admirals, reflecting the increased importance of new
politico-military tasks which involve high-ranking personnel. There

is an increase of generals in the army publication (7 to 20 per cent), but the navy has remained relatively stable (7 to 9 per cent).

RANK AND AUTHORSHIP

It can be argued that these trends are influenced by changes in the actual distribution of ranks during the period. This is not the case, as can be seen from the data on rank distribution in table 4. In the army the concentration of junior officers increased from roughly three-fifths to two-thirds, while their representation declined in the sponsored journal. The increase in contributions of general officers is not a result of their increased concentration. This figure remained stable between 1938 and 1959. With the noteworthy decline in concentration of flag officers, the distribution of ranks in the navy remained virtually unchanged and also constituted a pattern toward which the army moved.

A more direct method of presenting these data is to calculate an editorial quotient, namely, ratio of the percentage of published articles by holders of a given rank to that rank's representation in the army or navy officer corps for that period, as presented in table 5.

Table 4: Distribution of Rank: Army and Navy, 1938-1959[a]

Rank	1938		1948		1959	
	Per Cent	Number	Per Cent	Number	Per Cent	Number
Army						
Flag	.5	66	.6	348	.5	485
Field	41	5,138	34	22,811	35	31,812
Junior	58	7,310	66	50,301	64	58,322
Total	100[a]		100		100	
Navy						
Flag	01	83	.6	261	.5	299
Field	35	3,054	33	13,685	36	23,712
Junior	64	3,589	66	27,283	64	42,363
Total	100		100		100	

[a]Columns do not necessarily add to 100 per cent because of rounding.

Table 5: Trends in Editorial Quotient, 1938-1959

Rank	1938		1948		1959	
Army						
Flag	14	$\frac{.07}{.005}$	30	$\frac{.18}{.006}$	40	$\frac{.20}{.005}$
Field	1.29	$\frac{.53}{.41}$	2.09	$\frac{.71}{.34}$	1.57	$\frac{.55}{.35}$
Junior	.66	$\frac{.38}{.58}$	.09	$\frac{.06}{.66}$	.27	$\frac{.17}{.64}$
Navy						
Flag	5	$\frac{.05}{.01}$	15	$\frac{.09}{.006}$	18	$\frac{.09}{.005}$
Field	1.54	$\frac{.54}{.35}$	2.12	$\frac{.70}{.33}$	1.92	$\frac{.69}{.36}$
Junior	.59	$\frac{.38}{.64}$	.26	$\frac{.17}{.66}$	.30	$\frac{.19}{.64}$

These data confirm and amplify the foregoing conclusions. They highlight even more sharply the marked decline in the representation of junior officers in both services and point, in addition, to some recovery of representation in the last period as the services strive to find a new professional identity for junior personnel. The position of the middle-level field-grade officer is seen as more than stabilized; these measures clearly reveal an increase in prominence. Most noteworthy is that, by these measures, the upward trend in the representation of generals and admirals appears more pronounced.

These trends in frequency of appearance need to be related to the contents of articles. What shifts have occurred in the types of articles written by the different ranks? For the army, the data show that, in the earlier period, the junior officers wrote primarily narrow professional—technical—articles. As their prominence declined, the junior officers continued and even increased their concern with such articles. In short, there was a widening of the divergence between the professional model of the junior officer and that of the field-grade officer in ground force sponsored litera-ture. In the navy, by contrast, while junior officers were heavily involved in writing narrow professional articles, this type of writing did not predominate in the earlier period, nor did it increase with time. The junior naval officer had other professional images, since he wrote frequently about history and morale building, and even wrote broad professional articles; and this pattern has remained relatively stable through the period under investigation. In short, the model of the junior officer in the navy did not diverge so sharply from that of the field-grade officer.

The type of content the officer produces in sponsored literature is a measure of his professional self-image and of the competence the profession attributes to different ranks. Thus it appears that the army has been inclined to develop a professional identity in its junior officers, as if they were members of a distinct category with special responsibilities and special experiences, while the navy has treated its junior officers rather like apprentices to the roles of commanders and captains. In the army, the accomplishments of platoon leaders and company commanders are considered little more than "mere experience." By contrast, the experience of the junior officers seems to have general significance to the organizational and professional problems of the navy. In a sense, this is another expression of the navy's greater ability to fuse primitivist orientations into its competitive and managerial elements, since in the primitivist model the experiences of the junior officers are of concern to the organization as a whole.

For the field-grade officer in both services, the trend in content has been toward greater emphasis on conceptual materials, particularly in the areas of applied strategy. It is through the field-grade officers and civilians, rather than through the highest-ranking officers, that the professional issues of adjusting military means to national goals are discussed. But even at this middle-management level, a difference remains between the army literature and the navy literature. In the army, the number of field-grade officers concerned with historical material have sharply declined, while the number concerned with this continues in the naval journal. Again, the army's striving for a competitive and managerial model seems to allow less opportunity for reflection of past accomplishments as part of the professional model, while naval counterparts still make use of this preoccupation.

The closer a service approaches the managerial model, the more extensive, intense, and customary does the range of its interactions with the outside world become. Many of these contacts are encountered by the top-ranking generals and admirals, but these contacts also pervade the entire rank structure. It appears that top-ranking officers carry the editorial burden of writing or at least signing articles dealing with basic strategic, technical, and politico-military affairs. And it is true that their presence has increased, particularly in the army-sponsored literature. In a statistical sense they are overrepresented, but they are not and cannot become the most frequent contributors. If they did it would convert the sponsored communication into an assigned communication. They must rely on the middle-ranking officer, particularly the staff officer who has fuller command of the details, and on civilians as part of the process of managerial administration.

IMPORTANCE OF PROFESSIONAL WRITING
FOR CAREER ADVANCEMENT

It is possible to speculate about the importance of professional writing in sponsored channels for career advancement. Under the professional image of the older, heroic, and primitivist model, a common and universally applicable set of standards of military proficiency was assumed, and the demonstration of this proficiency was the basis for professional success. Contributions by an officer of any rank were designed to demonstrate mastery of his particular assignment and thereby his usefulness to the whole profession. Mastery in general, rather than the significance of the particular problems, was stressed. Professionalism was regarded as a capacity to cope with the problems of military life. A scheme for more effective garbage disposal merited as much space as an examination of the role of armored vehicles in modern warfare. The emphasis was on military duty as a unique way of life rather than on the armed forces as an instrument for coping with social and political problems.

Under these circumstances, it was considered desirable for a military officer to write for publication because it helped stress the universality of such standards and brought them to the attention of the broadest possible professional audience. Officers, junior and senior, hoped that their published writings would help their career advancement; not as innovators, however, but rather as individuals actively engaged in making established systems more efficient. The risk of deviancy was limited because the problems discussed were already well established as part of the institutional routine. Publication brought the author to the attention of important officers; it also demonstrated that he was devoting himself to the development of his overall competence rather than to the cultivation of specialized skills.

In terms of the competitive model, with its managerial outlook, the assumption is that every assignment has its own particular criteria of efficiency. Therefore, proficiency in a given assignment does not necessarily qualify an officer for promotion to another assignment. A variety of additional, often intangible, criteria become operative, such as the capacity for growth. The problems and approaches of one assignment may appear to have no direct relationship to those of its successor. Under these circumstances, publication becomes less a device for enhancing an officer's chances for promotion.

Sponsored literature in the new context is less concerned with stimulating individual contributions to general standards of proficiency. Publication is, rather, devoted to the dissemination of information in the interests of professional solidarity and group cohesion. The officer writes less to glorify his own particular assignment and more to educate and influence other officers involved in the processes of policy formation, coordination, and implementation.

Under the managerial model, general and flag officers contribute articles in order to educate one another and to inform the lower ranks about the complex problems which they know are being handled at higher levels and with which the lower ranks have no direct experience. Middle-grade officers contribute articles to demonstrate that they are applying the directives of their superiors to particular problems—but in a fashion which they hope is creative and not merely mechanical. Junior officers have fewer opportunities to apply such high-level principles. Therefore, they retain a residue of their traditional role of demonstrating that, notwithstanding the new emphasis on conceptual problems, there is still a place for a professional interest in purely technical matters and for concern with fundamental military values.

Our analysis has focused on content; but this is incomplete, since understanding the full significance of the contemporary sponsored literature involves an understanding of changes in the audience as well. The professional journal is typically addressed to other professionals, and in a sense to other specialists. This was true of *Infantry* and *U.S. Naval Institute Proceedings* before World War II. The shift toward the competitive model has also involved the development of multiple audiences. *Army* is edited in part for the benefit of the Association of the United States Army. The *U.S. Naval Institute Proceedings,* although to a lesser degree, tends to serve the interests of the more professionally minded members of the Naval League. (The Naval League has its own house organ, *Navy*.) Retired military personnel, university personnel concerned with defense establishment matters, and informed citizens are now audiences that must be addressed—but without losing the interest of the military professional.

In the pre-World War II period, sponsored journals stressing the history and narrow professional techniques of the service reinforced the professional sense of tradition and continuity. They provided a professional forum for the problems to be covered in future assigned literature—for example, field manuals. In writing a serious article for publication, the professional soldier was presenting his reflections upon the instructions which had been provided to guide him in performing his official duties. These reflections were useful for his peers and supplied information to higher-ranking officers about the strengths and weaknesses of the military system.

The newer publications continue to some extent to serve the same purposes, but unlike its earlier counterparts the contemporary journal is less committed to the exploration and improvement of official routine. This is perhaps because the framework of improvement has shifted from an arsenal to a laboratory model. New devices ranging from operational analysis to performance budgeting are now employed. The sponsored journal places a stronger emphasis on bringing to the officer's attention problems and procedures outside his normal professional pattern. The sponsored journal is at the frontier of the military establishment, indicating the areas where innovation is or should be in process rather than how it is being accomplished. For better or worse, the journal serves the military imagination rather than the military routine. The articles published in the old style of sponsored journal did not extend much beyond the doctrine and routine accepted and promulgated by the military service. The articles published in the managerially oriented journal are expected to open new and unexplored areas for military speculation and reflection.

The journals once operated, as the arsenal, for technical development. By contrast, managerially oriented publications are oriented toward exploring the innovative aspects of organizational experience at the level of doctrine and mission defining. They have become analogous to the laboratory type of developments. Laboratory developments, however, involve skills which, properly speaking, are not military. The professional engaged in them is only incidentally a member of some armed force. His contributions to the military journals are meant to popularize rather than stimulate his accomplishments.

In summary, we may speak of the transformation of the content and approach of sponsored military literature and use these materials to probe the basic changes in professional self-image in a technological environment. First, there is the underlying change that pervades both services as they move from a primitive self-conception to a competitive or managerial orientation. In simplest terms, the old model of sponsored literature was a professional journal written by and for military personnel. It was a journal in which field-grade officers predominated, but where junior officers also had an important role. In its content, historical and narrow professional—technical—articles were as important as conceptual articles. The newer approach is that of a journal in which specialists write for the edification of the general professional community as well as for all interested members of the general lay public. While the field-grade officer still predominates, the junior officer has declined markedly. Civilian contributions have grown in prominence; papers by high-ranking officers appear more frequently. Historical and narrow technical articles have declined, while the broad conceptual articles, dealing with applied strategy and civil-military issues, set the basic element of the self-image.

Second, the divergence between the services is an important as the basic pattern of change. The naval journal clearly indicates that the process of change had started for the navy before World War II. The army, when confronted with the realities of change, fluctuated more sharply toward the competitive model during the post-World War II period, while the navy continued its process of gradual change. Thus, as of 1959, the navy had developed a model which was basically committed to the competitive and managerial approach but embodied important and clear-cut elements of the primitive approach, while the army still was seeking a fusion of the traditional military heroic self-conceptions with contemporary politico-military requirements. If the service journals are a relevant indicator, the navy has undergone a less radical change in professional self-image than the army. The navy has followed a pattern of increased professionalization by stimulating conformity to existing patterns while modifying them slowly. The army has engaged in a drastic and unstable search for new bases of professional identity.

Postscript:

The research for this paper was drawn from an analysis, at ten year intervals, of journal contents, all when the U.S. armed forces were not engaged in overt hostilities. For this reason it was impossible to bring this article up to date for the late 1960's. Recent research, viz. Abercrombie, Clarence L., III and Major Raoul H. Alcalá, "The New Military Professionalism," in Bruce M. Russett & Alfred Stepan, *Military Force and American Society,* Harper and Row, 1973, pp. 34-68, tends to bear out my original hypotheses. Their analysis of the U.S. Army journal over the period 1940-1970 revealed a steady rise in the politicization of contents and the progressive atrophy of the characteristic contributions of company grade officers.

Chapter 5

PROFESSIONALISM, NATIONALISM, AND

THE ALIENATION OF THE MILITARY

I

The sociology of the military profession is, in essence, the study of an elite group. It is a political elite, moreover, functioning as such by virtue of the roles it plays within the society of nations and within its own social structure: that of being a key instrument of international conflict and that of being the ultimate arbiter upon occasions of extreme internal disorder.

This is not to assert that the soldier is a purely political animal, devoid of social and economic motivations. The rewards of his calling—in this paper I am dealing exclusively with members of the officer class—include wealth and status as well as power. The authoritative position of the officer is, however, based on the political utility of the organization he directs. Before everything else, he is a public servant. As in all other walks of life, wealth and status may facilitate entrance into and success throughout a chosen career. High rank, in return, normally results in a notable increment in status and wealth. But

Reprinted from Armed Forces and Society: Sociological Essays, *ed. by Jacques van Doorn, 1968, pp. 55-70.* © *Mouton Publishers.*

such considerations apply only to individuals. For the officer corps as a whole, what really determines prestige is the role played within the political life of the nation. Everything else—desirability as a profession, attractiveness of rewards—follows from that.

This narrow attachment to the factor of political power has its price. The range of rewards and inducements of a military career are limited by the fact that military service is a public monopoly. Within his social system, the organization he belongs to is the only one to which the soldier can legitimately sell his skills. His bargaining position is a limited one. Unlike most other professionals, he is not confronted by a variety of economic institutions and particular communities competing for his special talent. He can take advantage of other opportunities, but only by shedding his professional status, resigning his commission, and adopting a civilian career.

Another way of putting this is to assert that the military officer represents a case of purely *ascriptive professionalism*. His particular role is the direct result of his active membership and assigned position in a special organization. His professional status is subject to a continual process of review and reassessment. While terminal limits do exist, there is really no guaranteed age of retirement. He is liable to dismissal back into the civilian world whenever the organization considers his usefulness to have come to an end.

Ascriptive professionalism means that career decisions are entirely in the hands of the organization and that tenure-like considerations play virtually no role. Background and training may be pertinent data in the process of role selection, but it is the official act of selection and designation itself which confers the label of professionalism on the individual soldier. It is not enough to be a member of a particular social class or to have graduated from a special school. The status opportunities inherent in the latter situations may be conferred or withheld, depending upon the usefulness to the organization of the individual in question. The ability to fill some organizational requirement may, of itself, be enough to lead to the granting of promotions and commissions to individuals otherwise academically untrained and socially unqualified. Officer status is a result of organizational fiat and may be withdrawn as arbitrarily as it is conferred.

Ascriptive professionalism accordingly guarantees an exceptional degree of dependence upon and therefore of loyalty to the organization by its individual members. The loyalty and dependence are not, however, undivided. The relationship of the officer to the armed forces is balanced by an analogous relationship between the armed forces and the state. Here again the relationship is one of status dependency. Just as the individual soldier depends upon the organization for the legitimization of his rank, armed aggregates are dependent upon political sponsorship for their recognition as conventional armed forces. According to rules of international law, an armed force is as professional as its government is legitimate.[1] In other professions the status of already accredited or of candidate members depends more or less on the manner in which they perform their particular roles and not on or for whom. In the military business, the authority of a particular armed force to confer professional status is directly dependent upon the degree of international acceptance its government enjoys. Without such acceptance, its members are no more than disturbers of the peace. Experience or reputation, no matter how extensive, cannot give professional status to an armed band lacking a recognized political sponsor.

Military success does, of course, lead to political authority, and political authority generally results in international recognition. The victorious rebels become the legitimate state. But the claim of legitimacy and the right to possess and employ instruments of violence resides in the political sponsor and not in its armed forces. The leader of the army becomes the head of the state and appoints his own military successor and subordinate. The political and international influence of armed forces can thus normally be described as an expression of *surrogate authority*.

These two concepts of ascriptive professionalism and surrogate authority can be treated as the defining terms of military careerism. They fix both the limits and sources of power. The latter concept is as significant as the first, for the soldier has not only a profession but also a career. His possibilities of advancement are dependent not merely upon his own efforts but also upon the scope of opportunities his organization offers. This in turn depends upon the strength and stability of the state and upon the posture the state is willing and able to take in domestic and international affairs.

For all this formal dependence, the state-armed forces relationship might appear to be a one-sided one. With their near monopoly of the instruments of violence and with their control of a highly disciplined organization designed to employ them, the officer corps would appear to possess an almost limitless capacity to force the state and its policies into the forms they consider most favorable to their own interests. Surrogate authority might, paradoxically, be said to encourage an active military role in political life.

But this possibility is, with equal paradox, balanced, at least theoretically, by the concept of ascriptive professionalism. The extreme dependence upon his organization of the individual officer enables the organization to impose upon its members its own standards of professional attitudes and professional behavior. Armed forces are enmeshed in a tangle of rules and traditions defining both what is proper for them as soldiers and what is moral for them as servants of the state. Central to this control mechanism is the assertion that the management of violence is to be used only for politically approved purposes.[2]

But what "politically approved purposes" are is not always easily determined. Within the framework of the state, authority may be incoherently divided, policies inadequately or not at all formulated, and the process of succession inoperative or ambiguous. The open defiance of the government by groups other than the armed forces may put in question not only the goverment's ability to maintain order but also its right to direct a society which its very existence seems to divide.

There are, of course, general rules. It is usually considered both proper and moral for an armed force to wage war following the wishes of the government in power, and improper and immoral for it to engage in such hostilities upon its own initiative. Within the more complicated domestic arena, it is usually proper and moral for an armed force to aid the established government in the suppression of disorders which seem to threaten the stability of society, but improper and immoral in such a situation to take, without explicit authorization, the side of either government or opposition.

When applied to actual cases, however, these criteria appear to be inadequate guides. Even external war, which in appearance is simpler, offers many examples of conflict. The verdict of contemporary history is that de Gaulle and Kemal Ataturk[3] were justified, one in continuing and the other in starting a war, when in both instances the regime in power had ordered the reverse. But in analogous cases, the French generals in Algeria in 1961 and the Japanese officers in Manchuria in 1931 have been judged to have behaved both improperly and immorally. Nevertheless strong moral grounds have been attributed to the former[4] and cogent professional reasons to the latter.[5] Similarly, the German officer corps have been condemned for not offering greater resistance to Hitler's aggressive plans, though their professional obligations were in this case quite clearly fulfilled.

Domestic intervention also has its complications. In Egypt and Pakistan the armed forces ousted the constitutional regimes and in doing so appear to have created more stable and popular governments. On the other hand, the military coup of 1943 in Argentina, though ousting an already discredited regime, subjected that nation to a cycle of ineffective government and military intervention from which it has yet to emerge; and the Venezuelan military coup of 1948 resulted in ten politically and socially disastrous years. The examples cited, moreover, have reasonably clear consequences. But the problem is made more complicated if we take into account the large number of countries where the verdict has yet to come in.

This chapter, however, will not deal with the grounds for either justifying or condemning such military acts. The cases mentioned above have been used solely to indicate the sort of tensions to which the combination of ascriptive professionalism and surrogate authority subjects the military officer. What is to be analyzed is the relationship of such tensions to the general political culture. To be more specific, what will be examined is the relationship between professional military standards and political activism. Does the existence of a self-regulating military system guarantee or jeopardize the stability of the state? My answers will, of course, be hypothetical and framed in terms of the light that mature societies cast upon the problems of emergent ones.

II

An unstable relationship between the professional soldier and his government has been described as a characteristic of "new nations."[6] The process of rapid change, it has been noted, creates an extreme degree of social instability and strain. Granting the validity of this hypothesis, one can nevertheless make the paradoxical observation that one of the salient features of new nations is that in a relative sense their recent history has been characterized by stagnation rather than transformation. Compared to so-called industrial societies, their social and economic structure has for the last hundred years exhibited a rather modest degree of transformation. If they do seem at present to be in a stage of radical development, it is perhaps because the events of recent years furnish such a sharp contrast with the stagnation of their immediate history.

Nevertheless, if we take examples from "advanced" societies, there is an apparent validity to the contention that civil-military tension and rapid social change are related. Consider the evidence of the recent past. Over the period 1860-1960, there were six major worlds powers: France, Germany, Great Britain, Japan, Russia, and the United States. All six were also in the forefront of industrialization. In terms of our two variables, they present the following pattern (see table 1).

Table 1: 1860-1960

	Civil-military tension	Social change
France	high	low
Germany	high	high
Great Britain	low	high
Japan	high	high
Russia	?	high
USA	low	high

The determinations in this table are obviously impressionistic, but they do fit in with general historical conventions. One of the examples, that of Russia, will be excluded from consideration for reasons of its unique political history. The remainder provide us with the following pattern: two nations, Germany and Japan, with a *high* degree of civil-military tension and a *high* degree of social change; two nations, Great Britain and the United States, with a *low* degree of civil-military tension and a *high* degree of social change; one nation, France, with a high degree of civil-military tension and a *low* degree of social change. To simplify our analysis, the discussion will be largely restricted to the three examples for which analytical material is most abundant:[7] France, Germany, and the United States. Using their histories as evidence, I will sketch several broad hypotheses as to the relationship between surrogate authority, ascriptive professionalism, civil-military relations, and social change.

Let us begin with the problem of civil-military relations. Was there any particular attitude toward society shared by the members of the three professional groups in question? The works of Demeter, Girardet, and Huntington, our most authoritative historical surveys, strike the reader with their continual evocation of a military sense of social alienation. In the period between 1815 and World War II, members of the officer class were dominated by the consciousness of an estrangement between their own way of life and the dominant social trends of their respective nations. In their eyes the major threat to the armed forces lay not in some hostile power but in the materialistic and leveling values of their own society.

The reaction to this threat was in each case unique. The conflict between officer and civil society was for the German officer corps a matter of their own deliberate choice. From the days of its Prussian eminence this group had pursued a policy of maintaining itself as a privileged and exclusive group, the embodiment of a unique and ultrapure set of social and political values. The organization's capacity for ascriptive professionalism was refined to a degree never attained before or since. Even though industrialization and national development had progressively reduced the aristocratic background of its membership, it continued to indoctrinate its new recruits in a tradition of anachronistic Junkerism and virulent anticivilianism. The German officer corps, even under the Nazis, regarded itself as a society above society and a state within the state. The primary loyalty of its members was not simply to the organization but more significantly to a kind of transcendental notion of personal honor and national mission. Society and government were, insofar as they failed to satisfy these nebulous terms, rejected as transitory and un-German.

In France, civil-military tension was also considerable and deliberate, but here the initiative can be said to have come more from the state than from its armed forces. Mindful of the national revolutionary tradition, successive governments attempted to keep the armed forces isolated and in a state of political and social inertia. The concept of surrogate authority was systematically imposed. The recruitment and promotion of officers were strongly influenced by the complexion of regimes. The soldier was assumed to be an instrument of order and of empire, indispensable for such purposes. His political and social beliefs were expected to be those of the class into which he had been born or with which he identified himself, not those of the profession he practiced. Whatever ideological bias the officer class displayed was focused upon the supranational issues of the threat of Germany and the preservation of the overseas empire.

The United States presents an interesting case in that the alienation of its military class cannot be described as being the result of ascriptive professionalism or of surrogate authority, of either autonomous intention or of imposed design. It just simply appears to have happened. Up until World War II there was not much attention given to either the social or the political significance of the professional officer. Historical factors may have played a part in this. Unlike France, whose modern history was generally felt to have begun with revolutionary and Napoleonic wars, or Germany, whose unity was popularly held to have been forged with "blood and iron," the history of the United States was essentially a civilian one. Its Revolutionary War had been a militia operation. The plantation South, the one society with a military tradition, had been effectively crushed in the Civil War. Subsequent armed conflicts had been neither professional in nature nor inspirational in effect. The accepted role of its armed forces was somewhat sanitary in nature, that of cleaning up infected areas. They were something in the way of unsuccessful private enterprises, publicly subsidized. Without either a supranational mission or a national role, the armed forces were relegated to passive obscurity.

These distinctions in the nature and degree of their social affiliation were accompanied by exhibited differences in the level of professional attainment. The consensus of informed opinion seems to be that the German officer corps, 1860-1940, was the most efficient of the major military establishments. The French officer corps was rated considerably lower, and the American military establishment considered to have scarcely been in the running.

It is perhaps significant to note that in terms of ascriptive professionalism and surrogate autority the German officer corps can be rated as strong in the first and weak in the second, the French the other way around, and the American rather neutral in both. Morover, an examination of the list of major powers of the first half of the twentieth century—France, Germany, Great Britain, Japan, Russia, and the United States—yield one serious rival to the German claims of professional military eminence, Japan. Here again, we find an officer corps strong in its professional identity and insubordinate to its civilian superiors.

I am not arguing that any army is better prepared for fighting a war through the fact of its being actively committed to some independent political position. The combination of professionalism and nationalism may result in a form of political surrealism that defeats its own ends. The examples here discussed are, anyhow, too limited in number and nature for the drawing of any definite conclusions. They all refer to events prior to 1940 and to societies exceptionally high on the scale of industrialization. What is being presented is the hypothesis that, in highly industrialized nations prior to 1940, the professional level of a particular military establishment was directly related to its conscious pursuit of an independent national role.

This, after all, is no more than some of the more prominent and sympathetic contemporary analyses of the political sociology of the military have claimed. Huntington has described the painful forging of an American professional military class through the gradual emergence of a sense of national mission; Demeter credits the eminence of the German officer corps to this factor and attributes its decline to the relinquishing of that role to the Nazi party. More significant because it is more contemporary, Girardet has credited the Algerian conflict with the creation of a French army far superior in professional effectiveness and political commitment to any in recent history and finds a bitter irony in the doubly foredoomed nature of that achievement.[8] All three authors have found military effectiveness to reside in a sense of distinctiveness not only about professional identity but also in the possession of a unqiue social role.

The particular relevance of this to present-day problems lies in the fact that it has become customary to regard the armed forces as an especially effective instrument in programs of social and economic modernization. Much more frequently than in mature societies, the problems of emergent nationhood are held to justify the active intervention of military leaders in the domestic political process. The armed forces regard themselves and are broadly supported as the unique embodiment of national unity. But are there reasonable historical grounds for regarding them as effective agents of national unification? Among the armed forces of "advanced" nations, where the concept of a unique national mission was both strong and explicit, the professional soldier seems to have been equally conscious of his membership in an unrepresentative, "alienated" group.[9]

III

Ascriptive professionalism and militant nationalism[10] are not necessarily inseparable. There are a large number of states where the military forces were highly professional in composition but nationally uncommitted, where officer corps were made up of international careerists, bound solely to the sovereign, and there by a contractual relationship.[11] On the other hand, there are examples of forces of a definitely unprofessional nature but with a strong sense of national mission, militia bands led by local worthies and destined to spontaneous dissolution upon the attainment of their objectives. But in the Western would these two kinds vanished by the mid-nineteenth century, disappearing with the emergence of the notion of the secular society. Henceforth, in the nations under consideration, we find armed forces whose degree of professionalization marches hand in hand with the self-conscious assumption of a national role.

Is this relationship an accidental one? It can perhaps be explained by treating the process of modernization as one in which accepted political goals are transformed from *absolutist* into *secular* ones. "In a secular society the essential purpose of political action is the improvement of the level of living of the citizens."[12] In an absolutist society the essential purpose of political action is that of increasing the internal control and external influence of the sovereign authority.[13] According to the secular ideology, public servants are participants in a commonly shared enterprise. Following the logic of absolutism, public servants are instruments of the particular goals of the sovereign. Given a general consensus on secularization, the professional soldier finds himself in an anomalous position. His is perhaps the only prominent group excluded both by tradition and by design from making a positive welfare contribution. His professional affiliation commits him to the absolutist concept of the state. By tradition the officer corps is anticommercial, non-entrepreneurial. In function it is nonproductive.[14]

On the other hand, the armed forces participate in the general expansion of industrial technology. The competitive experience of warfare forces even the most traditionally minded armies to take a more modern view of their responsibilities. The social and economic activities surrounding them cannot be ignored. Secularism and industrialism have created a new technology which emphasizes expertise at the expense of tradition.[15] The military have been modernized in spite of themselves. The criteria of military professionalism are now measured against the standards employed in secular enterprises.

My first hypothesis then is that the secularization of society has intensified both the professionalism and the alienation of the military. It has obliged the armed forces to adopt more rigid criteria for the selection and training of their officers. Ascriptive professionalism has thereby been emphasized. Simultaneously, the social basis for military privilege, i.e., the distinction between noblemen and commoners, has been progressively eliminated. The differentiation of soldiers and civilians has increasingly become a function of the armed forces themselves and not of society in general. But as secularization and industrialization spread, as expertise replaces tradition, the ascriptive processes discard absolutistic standards in favor of secular ones. The officer corps is forced to adapt itself to the criteria and practices of other professions. The soldier becomes more subject to the control of his organization and is at the same time informed that the honorific traditions of this organization no longer carry much weight. The expectation emerges that military policy should in some significant sense be a rational extension of social policy. At the same time, it is dogmatically denied that the armed forces have any particular social contribution to make. As a result the officer comes to consider himself as exploited by a society from which he is debarred.

My second hypothesis is that the military process of mutually reinforcing professionalization and alienation inclines the officer corps toward doctrines of militant nationalism. Wherever circumstances permit, military officers deny the existence of any special commitment to society on their part. They assert themselves to be bound by a unique allegiance to the state, to a constitution, or to a national tradition rather than to any particular regime; to concepts, in other words, which because they are permanent and unchanging have a stronger claim to loyalty than the secular procession of designedly transient and evolutionary regimes. This doctrine has the additional virtue of providing a traditionalist content to the otherwise increasingly secularized process of ascriptive professionalism. It offers the organization a basis for indoctrinating and assessing its members in terms which are purely its own.

The uses of militant nationalism serve as a partial explanation for the sympathetic approach to fascism displayed by significant numbers of professional soldiers during the period between the two world wars.[16] Fascism offered a vision of a modern society in which secular welfare and sovereign authority would be reconciled. The consciousness of a unique national mission would promote internal harmony, eliminate social conflict, and promote economic efficiency. The resultant increase in material wealth would enable the state more vigorously to pursue its rightful international role. Successful international adventures would provide the resources for raising the internal standard of living to a yet higher level.

Moreover, the authoritarian, one-party state would put an end to the domestic interplay of political factions and particular interest groups. In doing this, it would eliminate the condition of military alienation. With every form of political activity forbidden, the apolitical soldier would simply participate in a common national fate. With society organized in paramilitary terms, his special gifts would be particularly appreciated. His apolitical discipline would be a model for all.

The major drawback to this solution was that it was a purely imaginary one. It was guided by the old absolutist concept. By the twentieth century, the absolutist concept of the state had ceased to play a significant role in the Western world. In totalitarianism, the military saw a reemergence of the traditional supremacy of political authority over social conflict. But here they misread the evidence. The new authority did not intend to take a position above society. They sought to pervade it and to fuse the political and social structures into one system. The military offered their loyal services. But it was commitment, not service, that was demanded. There were to be no special cases. The totalitarian party and its leaders saw no justification for the existence of any independent professional groups. The military imagined that their profession's unique degree of professional expertise and national commitment would make them an exception. All their professionalism achieved was to make them particularly suspect. In the context of the totalitarian state, ascriptive professionalism and surrogate authority were more than anachronisms. They were heresies, positions vis-á-vis the established order which one side or the other was bound to find impossible to maintain.

Under any circumstances there were bound to be difficulties.

There is a definite ambiguity to both the concept of ascriptive professionalism and that of surrogate authority. Both soldiers and civilians accept them as valid descriptions of the military outlook and of its conditions of service. But for the two parties the terms do not have the same meaning. For the soldier, ascriptive professionalism means that the armed forces remain above politics. To the civilian, secularist or totalitarian, ascriptive professionalism means that the political loyalty of the military is guaranteed. Both regard ascriptive professionalism as a guarantee of objectivity. But for the soldier this means that military decisions are to be made in a purely military setting, while to the civilian it implies that the soldier simply obeys orders. For the soldier the concept of surrogate authority means that the armed forces are to be free to follow their own unique set of values and that the civilian and military spheres should be sharply delimited. For the civilian it represents the precautionary isolation of a potentially unreliable group, and this implies that military activities be kept in a condition where they can be constantly and closely observed.

This conflict of interpretations finds its most clear-cut expression in the question of the relationship between the professional soldier and the nation-state. Soldiers and civilians agree that ascriptive professionalism and surrogate authority are the premises of the modern military condition. They differ about how the attitudes in question can be resolved into a valid social role.[17] For the officers, militant nationalism represents the logical solution. For the civilian, depolitization is the obvious answer. Each side believes itself to possess an obvious and easy answer. But what is satisfactory to one group violates all the principles of the other. In nations such as Great Britain and the United States, where the secular persuasion is dominant, the armed forces are, by and large, inert and apolitical. In states such as Japan and Germany, where the absolutist tradition had a strong hold, the pursuit of doctrinaire nationalist programs committed the armed forces to an active political life and at the same time underminded and eventually destroyed the secular order. In France, which for a century and a half lay stranded between the two ideologics, the officer corps was divided within itself in the intermittent practice of these two roles and contributed in significant part to the torpor and inertia which characterized the political life of that nation.

In all three examples, the solutions finally arrived at accurately reflect the internal politics of the nations involved. An apolitical officer corps is a direct consequence of a stable political order. An actively nationalist professional military body is a symptom of deteriorating or ineffective civilian rule. Militant nationalism is, in its way, the objective correlative of military alienation, the practical analogue of a psychological state. Its programmatic ends correspond to its inner sense of unbridgeable social divisions. The aim of militant nationalism is political stability. But it is the stability of a vacuum, a state undisturbed by the erratic movements of partisan bodies. My third hypothesis, therefore, can be expressed in the following form: Since the military policy of a secular society has as its objective the creation of an apolitical armed force, and the social policy of the professional soldier has as its objective the creation of an apolitical society, sustained and equal partnership between the two is impossible.

IV

For the moment let us accept the assertion that in modernizing societies civil-military relations actually do fall into the pattern described above. Is this inevitably so? Must other nations following the path of modernization suffer the same experience? Most new nations have adopted the secularist goals of improving the general level of living. Many of them regard their armed forces as important instruments in the achievement of this end. Is commitment to a secularist political approach without a resultant alienated officer corps possible?

There is considerable evidence for the contention that the incidence of alienation is a peculiar condition, that in much of recorded history and in many contemporary nations it did not occur. Indeed, it can be argued that in most nations the military occupy or have occupied a secure and honored position. The decline in military status exists only in a comparative sense. In most cases the professional soldier is still a member of an acknowledged elite.

Is military alienation then a necessary consequence of rapid social change? Modern society has been described as a condition where the conflict of social groups is assumed to be mutually beneficial in both material and moral terms.[18] The armed forces suffer because there is a strain in them which represents a notable exception to this statement. Somewhere the belief persists that "there is really no substitute for victory." They can and do compete, of course, but at the price of adapting themselves to civilian modes and rules. As a result they are the one major political group suspicious of the going rules of the game and suspected by the other participants. Their successful participation seems somehow to imply a radical transformation, the substitution of discipline for discussion and of hierarchy for compromise.

In a way, then, the military condition in a secular society is an anomalous one. As a class they are alienated because they cannot compete. And they cannot compete because in code and structure they are too different from the rest of society. Conflict which in other instances is assumed to reinforce social integration does in their case become an act too radical to be safely managed. The historical conditions of their successful integration presuppose a society in which leadership in the armed forces is synonymous with membership in the political and social elite or else one in which the structure of authority is so monolithic as to reduce internal competition to an exceptionally low level.[19]

It is not entirely true that the professional soldier is incapable of competing in the politics of modern state. The price, however, demanded for such behavior seems to be somewhat too high to be openly discussed. The professional soldier is most likely to enter into politics under the banner of a nationalistic program which proclaims the need for suspending much or most of secular competitive activity and for uniting the nation in the face of some extraordinary internal or external threat. Riding into power upon such a program, he faces the grave problem of knowing how and when to dismount, or of being able to establish some operational criteria for conclusively resolving the crises which led to his assumption of power. In either case, abdication is an extremely difficult and rare occurrence. If it is an external threat which has justified political action, then military victory may end the emergency and permit the resumption of normal political life. If, however, the threat is conceived to be internal, the possibilities of a return to secular politics are greatly diminished. The aspects of military alienation described above are likely to intensify rather than diminish the internal divisions which initially justified the seizure of power. The military themselves may become more secular-minded, but their regime is not likely to develop into a broader form of political consensus. The secularization of their own authority is likely to take place at the expense of civilian groups with whom they would "normally" have to compete. At best it may result in a solidification of civilian opposition and a resolution by nonmilitary groups that this crisis once over they will never again allow their differences to go so far as to create an opportunity for armed intervention. But this itself represents an inhibition of the secular process.

Given the current tendency towards the secularization of politics, the problem of military alienation may, in fact, be an insoluble one. Except for the extremity of total war and for the two or three states for whom this macabre condition represents a political alternative, the professional soldier has been reduced to a role which the value structure of his society categorizes as being both marginal and dysfunctional. In an incrementally minded situation he does not appear to have any positive contribution to make.

Among many of the "new nations" this fact has been recognized, and efforts have been made to reconstruct the professional military along new lines. The manipulation of violence has been deemphasized, and a special stress has been placed on the discipline and rational structure of military organization. The armed forces have been cast in a new light as an official instrument particularly well suited for the mobilization of national energies toward the attainment of high-priority social and economic goals. The military in these cases have been treated as a substitute, temporary or otherwise, for a high-level career in civil service.

It is noteworthy that the states in which this process is supposed to be taking place are by most indices just entering upon the process of secularization. They have assumed programs of development and are guided by models which have little direct relationship to their own social structure, programs and models which have been adopted precisely because their sponsoring societies have up to now made so little progress in the direction of secularization.

In these states the professional military are being called upon to undertake the direction of a process which would have as one of its ultimate results the creation of a social structure in which the political guidance would be entirely civil in origin. It is rather far-fetched to imagine a high-status social class rationally and willingly directing the process of its superannuation. But this, if it should ever turn out to be the case, would be the highest possible tribute to the professionalism of the armed forces.

NOTES

1. L. Oppenheim, *International Law*, Vol. 2; H. Lauterpacht, ed., *Disputes, War and Neutrality*, 8th ed. (London: Longmans, Green, 1955), pp. 248-268.
2. S. P. Huntington, *The Soldier and the State* (Cambridge, Harvard University Press, 1957), pp. 14-16.
3. Bernard Lewis, *The Emergence of Modern Turkey* (London and New York: Oxford University Press, 1961), pp 237-249.
4. George A. Kelly, *Lost Soldiers: The French Army and Empire in Crisis, 1947-1962* (Cambridge: MIT Press, 1965).
5. Takehiko Yoshihashi, *Conspiracy at Mukden* (New Haven: Yale University Press, 1963).
6. Edward Shils, "The Military in the Political Development of the New States," in *The Role of the Military in Underdeveloped Countries*, ed. J. J. Johnson (Princeton, N.J.: Princeton University Press, 1962), pp 7-68.
7. The following books have been used as background material for the statements made in the subsequent pages: F. L. Carsten, *The Reichswehr and Politics, 1918-1933* (London and New York: Oxford University Press, 1966); K. Demeter, *The German Officer Corps in Society and State, 1650-1945* (New York: Praeger, 1965); R. Girardet, *La Société Militaire dans la France contemporaine (1815-1939)* (Paris: Plon, 1953); R. Girardet, ed., *La Crise militaire Française 1945-1962* (Paris: A. Colin, 1964); Huntington, *The Soldier;* Morris Janowitz, *The Professional Soldier* (Glencoe, Ill.: Free Press of Glencoe, 1960); Kelly, *Lost Soldiers.*
8. Girardet, *Crise militaire,* pp. 173-185; 221-229.
9. The question is too complicated for discussion in this limited paper. But there appear to be cogent grounds for arguing that the military exacted an exorbitant price for their role in the unification of Germany. See L. B. Namier, *1848: The Revolt of the Intellectuals* (New York and London: Oxford University Press, 1946).
10. Being too significant a phenomenon to be described in negative terms, a weak degree of surrogate authority will henceforth be referred to as "militant nationalism."
11. Consider the career of the Prussian military hero, Marshall Blücher. Born in Rostock in 1742, he entered Swedish service in 1756. He was taken prisoner by the Prussians in 1760 and was persuaded to enter their service.

12. J. Fourastié, *The Causes of Wealth* (Glencoe, Ill.: Free Press of Glencoe, 1960), p. 21.

13. F. Meinecke, *Machiavellianism* (New Haven: Yale University Press, 1957), pp. 1-3.

14. "What, then, is the use of the *shi,* or *samurai,* class? Its only business is to preserve, or maintain, *giri* (right, honor, duty). The people of the other classes deal with visible things, while *samurai* deal with invisible, colorless, and insubstantial things . . . . If there were no *samurai,* right (*giri*) would disappear from human society, the sense of shame would be lost, and wrong and injustice would prevail." Tokugawa Mitsukini (1628-1700) to his samurai. Quoted, from an article by Ernest W. Clement in the *Transactions and Proceedings of the Japan Society* (London, 1898), by R. W. Bellah, *Tokugawa Religion* (Glencoe, Ill.: The Free Press of Glencoe, 1957), p. 90.

15. Janowitz, *Professional Soldier,* pp. 21-31.

16. Alfred Vagts, *A History of Militarism* (New York: Meridian, 1959), pp. 410ff.

17. A distinction should at this point be made between secularist and totalitarian attitudes with regard to the military. Secularism tends to further the military process of ascriptive professionalism; totalitarianism tends to politicize and prescribe the qualifications of military officers.

18. Lewis Coser, *The Functions of Social Conflict* (Glencoe, Ill.: Free Press of Glencoe, 1956), esp. pp. 70-81.

19. See chapter 2, this book.

Chapter 6

MASS ARMIES AND THE PROFESSIONAL

SOLDIER

The nature and origins of military professionalism constitute a subject which goes beyond the narrow confines of military history. Social thinkers as disparate as Machiavelli[1] and Max Weber[2] have seen the opening wedge of social policy in the problem of providing a rational basis for the construction and maintenance of armed forces, i.e., the systematic effort of sovereign authorities to employ the powers of the state to create from among its members the types of citizens it considered essential to its efficient functioning. For Weber, the professional soldier is the prototype of the bureaucratic functionary. For Machiavelli, the member of the civic militia is the ideal of the active citizen. For both, programmatically organized military service is the initial step in the creation of the modern state.

In both we find the creation of military institutions presented as the antithesis of the premodern state, a condition where social roles were determined either by local tradition or by the narrow imitation of the institutions of more successful societies. Prior to the modern era, a European state deficient in military or administrative talent would import it from abroad. The church and the nobility were at such times a floating international

Reprinted from the journal Armed Forces and Society, *Volume I, No. 2 (Winter 1975).*

reservoir of these skills.[3] In the modern state citizens are regarded as a unique resource and systematically trained in the skills the ruling structure considers necessary for its effective operation. The citizen is not simply a member of society: he is, to a significant degree, the creation and servant of its institutions.

Historically, however, the concepts of the professional officer and of the civic militia have had markedly different fates. From the moment of its adoption in the Netherlands in 1585, the concept of the professional officer was successful and became the prerequisite of military capability. The civic militia, on the other hand, was a disastrous failure in its initial application in Florence in the early sixteenth century and was not seen again until the mass armies of the French Revolution, after which it became the military sine qua non. This essay will attempt to explain and relate the immediate success of the one and the delayed acceptance of the other.

I

Let us begin by defining our key terms.

"Mass army" implies an armed force designed to attain the closest practical enrollment of the totality of the available manpower resources of the state in question. The reference to "mass," then, is not simply a function of size. The Israeli army of June 1967 was a mass army. In numbers, however, it was smaller than either the French or West German military of this period, neither of which can be described as a mass army.[4]

"Military professionalism" refers to an officer class conforming to a model according to which the recruitment, training, and assignment of its members are carried out entirely in terms of internally formulated criteria. It is best understood in opposition to a nonprofessional officer class, which can be defined as one where these processes are more or less determined by the ideological and social biases of the dominant political system. One thesis of this essay is that professionalism, i.e., the emergence of objective criteria for the management of the officer corps—

education and experience as opposed to birth and social position—
was a radical innovation, and that, once institutionalized, it
provided the rationalizing impetus for the acceptance of the mass
army.

Although my emphasis will be on military factors, it is essential
to realize that in these developments the political and the military
are virtually inseparable. The conduct of war is governed by the
nature of the political entities involved. Political revolutions
therefore have military consequences. The concept of military
professionalism first emerged in the Netherlands in 1585 in the
course of revolt against the Hapsburg monarch.[5] The critical role
of the emergent Dutch Republic in creating the notion of military
professionalism is an integral part of the process whereby that
state came into being. It was, at least in Western Europe, the
earliest case of sustained popular revolt against an acknowledgedly
legitimate authority—popular, that is, in the sense that the
rebelling group included and came to be dominated by representatives of the nonaristocratic classes.[6]

This casting off of legitimate authority had far-reaching
consequences. Before that time war had theoretically been
regarded as an exceptional *event*, justified insofar as it represented
an effort by the sovereign power to suppress disturbances, internal
or external, of the natural order.[7] It was conducted by members
of a particular class, the nobility, who by virtue of that function
were absolved from all other social responsibility. War in the
Dutch experience became a self-justifying process whereby a
hitherto legitimate system was overthrown and another painstakingly created to take its place.[8] The conduct of the war was one of
the various socially regulative functions the new ruling body had
to assume.

The revolt of the Netherlands thus seems to have coincided with
a crucial transformation of enlightened opinion. Erasmus
(1466-1536), the most eminent prerevolutionary Dutch man of
letters, considered warfare the antithesis of the practices of civil
society. It was, at best, a case of fighting fire with fire. He
regarded the soldier as a monster who stood outside of society and
preyed upon it. Military virtues, if they could so be described,
were seen as completely antithetical to the precepts of Christianity

and the laws of society.[9] The most eminent Dutch scholar of the second half of the sixteenth century, Justus Lipsius (1547-1606), saw matters in exactly opposite terms, asserting that the traits leading to military proficiency were the epitome and basis of all virtue, the foundation of political and social order.[10] In the seventeenth century Lipsius was probably the most widely read and translated of philosophers. His works, both ethical and political, were the standard texts in the universities created by post-Reformation rulers for the express purpose of training civil servants for the emergent bureaucratic systems.[11]

The Dutch experience was one where the creation of an armed force and the creation of a state were simultaneous and unprecedented acts. The necessity of creating stable and effective institutions virtually from nothing gave a radical perspective to the outlook of individuals otherwise traditionally inclined. The leaders of the emergent Dutch army became military professionals through the enforced realization—spared commanders in more established states—that armed forces were not a conventional part of the traditional social order, but especially designed instruments of specific social and political policies. They must, therefore, be regarded as social bodies made up of individuals standing in a special relationship to one another and joined together for the achievement of specific ends. Once this fact had been recognized, precise standards of performance had to be articulated and special skills developed for and applied to attaining them. The professional officer came into being, indoctrinated in the necessity of maintaining these standards and trained in the procedure of achieving them.[12]

The mass army can be regarded as the historical consequence of the transformation of this insight into a doctrine and of its being carried to its extreme conclusion. If armies are social bodies, wars are conflicts between societies. The victor would thus be the society best able to mobilize and organize its resources. In the process of transformation, a peculiar inversion occurred. The idea that armed forces were actually societies led to the belief that societies could be armed forces. The realization that a quasi-legislative code could be drafted for the formation and control of effective armies[13] culminated in the policy of having a legal and administrative system to exploit the entirety of society's resources for military ends. The search for skills and techniques specifically designed for rationalizing warfare developed into the practice of studying every socially proven technique of the armed state. Truck drivers, TV personalities, professors, artists, and poets all had their appropriate niches in the mobilized society.

My second argument is then quite simple. As a vehicle of social policy the mass army is more than a military phenomenon. It is, in effect, the expression of a collective myth. The notion of the general strike was designed to produce a sentiment of solidarity among laborers, overcome fragmented outlooks, and create a unified working class. In the same way, the notion of general mobilization was designed to produce a similar sense of unity in society, erase individual differences, and make every inhabitant of the administered territory a citizen of the nation-state.[14]

The professionalization of military skills was the first instance of the political creation of a specific social group, the professional officer. The mass army can be regarded as the inverse of this: the politically inspired creation of an integrated society, the nation-in-arms. The emergence of the nation-state concept was an integral factor in this process. That it and the mass army invariably appear together is surely no accident. Before the French Revolution neither was to be found; afterward they sprang into being in a manner which makes it difficult to determine the sequence of creation. France in the process of becoming a nation-state invented the *levée en masse.* Prussia created a mass army and as a result brought the German nation-state into being. Italy celebrated her unification by instituting a system of universal military service. The mass army, with its concomitant administrative apparatus of universal military service, was the most striking and pervasive symbol of a new kind of politics. The state took a positive interest in the activities of every inhabitant—male inhabitant, that is—of its supervised territories, and the prospect of military service gave every inhabitant a more or less positive role in the state.[15]

"The levy in mass, the telegraph, and the income tax are all from France," wrote Robert Southey in 1807.[16] The relationship of the mass army with the concept of an all-pervasive and all-inclusive state was not lost on the witnesses of its emergence.

The very term *levée en masse* associated the general populance with the idea of active participation in the state. Conscription was as much a matter of social as of military policy. Military service and political rights were closely equated. According to the new political outlook, the ballot was the minimal political right and military service the basic civic obligation. The former was widely considered to be justified by the latter.[17] That is, military service represented a claim to full citizenship and was a conventional means whereby the disenfranchised gained civic rights.

The nineteenth-century acceptance of the mass army created the background for the rise of an officer class that was socially as well as procedurally self-determining. Prior to that time, the officer corps had been aristocratically dominated. Professional officers were accepted as individual specialists but not as integrated members of a corporate body whose admissions criteria were based on class. Officer corps of the period between the Dutch Revolt and the French Revolution had operated more or less on a two-tiered system.[18] Their fundamental component was drawn from the ranks of the nobility, and they were noblemen first and officers only incidentally. Noble descent was regarded as a guarantee both of loyalty to the crown and of heroic leadership. The second component of the officer corps comprised individuals possessing attainments not guaranteed by pedigree. These were primarily specialists—artillerymen and engineers—whose skills, largely mathematical, could be acquired only through intensive study. There was a certain amount of overlap, but basically these two orders stood in opposition to one another. Noble spirits could not be expected to enter into the laborious process of learning a trade, and an officer trained in the science of rational calculation was considered to be both potentially disloyal and fundamentally incapable of heroic abandon.[19]

The mass army by its very nature required officers addicted to the habits of numerical calculation. If the basic requirement of warfare was the most complete possible mobilization of the nation's resources, the basic leadership role had to be one of planning rather than of inspiration. Planning, moreover, involved coordination rather than heroic example. The pressures on the officer corps were therefore such as to make its members define themselves as members of a corporate body of trained specialists rather than as a collection of specially endowed and privileged individuals. In Western Europe, only Great Britain, the country least touched by the French Revolution, avoided conscription and retained the old military order.[20]

Nineteenth-century officer corps were, of course, essentially still drawn from the upper classes. Special preference was given to members of the nobility. But in those states supporting a mass army, objective standards were for the first time applied to all members of the officer corps. The upper classes were now on the defensive, paying lip service, at least, to factors other than birth and personal connections. The processes transforming armies and societies were altering the self-image of the military officer. If military service was to be justified as a process that converted passive individuals into active citizen-soldiers,[21] the officer corps could not escape the implications of its role as the agent of this conversion. Formerly a member of a self-justifying caste, one whose privileges were based on its claim of standing apart from and resisting the trends of society, the officer was now part of a bureaucratic system, a guardian of the national interest, an inculcator of the sense of civic duty, prepared at all times to preside over the rites of sacrifice required by the faith.

II

Both the professional officer corps and the mass army were products of a political revolution. Both can be regarded as the result of a specific social policy on the part of the state. Professional officers were the product of an effort to create a body of military leaders independent of the existing social structure; the mass army, the expression of an attempt to mobilize the forces of society into the service of the state. The professional officer, the creation of a narrow social policy, acted as the administrator of a more universal one.

Just as the bases for military professionalism were to be found in the conditions of revolt in the sixteenth-century Netherlands, the background for the mass army is to be found in the circumstances of the French Revolution. Prerevolutionary France was legally and administratively divided into three estates—the clergy, the nobility, and everyone else—representing respectively the church, the state, and society. The church was a quasi-independent corporation; the nobility effectively dominated the structure of military and public offices. Society, sharply differentiated from the state, was given the function of passively submitting to taxation—a burden from which the other two estates were exempted on the basis of the public services they performed.[22]

Underlying all this was a theory of privilege based on military conquest. The nobility were, in effect, the victoriously invading Franks; the commoners, the conquered Gallo-Romans. The ancien régime was, in the terms of its defenders, an order based on conquest: politics was the spoils system of the victorious invaders. Commoners were excluded not merely because they lacked the patent of nobility but, more fundamentally, because they were not considered members of the state.[23]

The revolutionaries were well aware of this. One of the earliest acts of the Constituent Assembly abolished aristocratic privilege in the armed forces (August 4, 1789, less than a month after the fall of the Bastille). One month later similar measures were put into effect for civil offices.[24] In summer 1789, moreover, the Third Estate had spontaneously organized its own army, the National Guard. Its accession to power was thus proclaimed by the creation of its own exclusively bourgeois armed force.[25]

Under the ancien régime military leadership had been an obligation of the aristocracy and enlisted service a free choice of the lower classes. Officers were, then, the elite of the political establishment, and enlisted men were a marginal low-status residue of society. The Revolution reversed this. The break with the established order created a class of officers whose service in the revolutionary army was a matter of deliberate choice. Further, in creating its army, the new state proclaimed military service to be a universal civic duty.[26]

This was, in effect, to assert: (1) that all members of society were henceforth to participate in the operations of the state; and (2) that the higher ranks were now to be a public profession open by free choice to all, regardless of birth. It was on this basis that the revolutionary armies were formed and the revolutionary national state was created.

Artillery and engineering officers were, as a group, enthusiastic supporters and special beneficiaries of this development. Within the officer corps of the ancien régime they had been considered a marginal body—technicians lacking the capacity for general command. The military revolution of the seventeenth century had created a demand for tactical and administrative skills that the traditional nobility had been unwilling or unable to supply. Military specialization had, as a result, become an avenue of entrance into the officer corps and therefore into the ranks of the nobility. Since noble status conferred both eligibility for political preferment and exemption from taxation, a military career, even of a marginal kind, was an obvious path of upward social mobility.[27]

The army, however, was the glorified sinecure system of the upper aristocracy. It was the only moneymaking profession most of its members could pursue. As the financial difficulties of the monarchy increased, the pressure from the upper aristocracy to limit admission into the officer corps increased. An ordinance of 1781 had restricted both entrance into the officer corps and promotion to the rank of general to individuals with at least four generations of noble descent. Further enactments in 1788 reserved the ranks of colonel upward for officers with either the highest grades of nobility or a noble pedigree dating back to at least 1400.[28]

The burden of retrenchment thus fell on officers who were members of the lesser nobility, of the rural gentry, or of the ascendant bourgeoisie. These individuals were concentrated in the technical branches where competition from the upper nobility was less intense and where the existence of objective criteria gave their ambitions some scope. The Revolution of 1789 gave them an opportunity to redress grievances and to compete for the highest grades. Large numbers of them entered the army of the Revolution. It is no accident that Carnot, the "Organizer of Victory," was an engineer and that Napoleon was an artillerist.

Two profound social transformations were brought about by

the French Revolution: (1) through the destruction of the system of estates, the division of society into political and nonpolitical classes was, in theory, eliminated; and (2) through the elimination of the ranks of nobility, every citizen was made eligible for public office. These were conscious changes; there was a third which, though unanticipated, was as far-reaching. The Revolution, in overturning what the other European rulers regarded as a natural and just order, not only put itself outside the family of nations but also assumed the proportions of a threat to its neighbors. From 1791 on, it was faced with the anticipated threats from within and with concerted attacks on its frontiers. Military defense thus became its overriding concern and the newly enfranchised citizen not only the beneficiary of its proceedings but also its major resource. The army had been the bulwark of the ancien régime and was therefore unreliable. It was replaced by a levée en masse from the newly liberated society, supplemented by a body of officers whose service was a matter of personal choice rather than of traditional vocation.

A combination of factors, therefore, led to the emergence of the first mass armies. A revolution made the highest offices in public life open to all, at a time when national defense was the major political problem. A social revolution asserted that every member of society had an interest in the state. A bureaucratic revolution abolished ascriptive qualifications and made professional capacity the determining factor in military assignments and promotions. This last can scarcely be exaggerated. It secured to the republic the loyalty of the most professional of French military officers and thereby gave the mass army a unique technocratic bias at a time when the rank and file were by any standard a raw, untrained mob. The Revolutionary Army was characteristically weak in calvary and strong in artillery and enthusiasm.

III

The revolutionary mass army was, however, an army of circumstance rather than a standing army. It was created to meet special situations and to fight particular campaigns. Ideology rather than technology kept it in the field. The attrition through disease and desertion was always heavy. In most cases, moreover, it can be argued that the victories gained were due more to the morale of the troops and the talents of the generals than to the weight of numbers. The levée en masse did give France the manpower to wage war on several fronts simultaneously. But the armies that waged particular campaigns were relatively small in number. Mass armies were used by Napoleon only in his later campaigns and, after Jena-Auerstadt (1806), the results were disastrously costly.[29]

The technical means of transporting, supplying, and coordinating the movements of a body of more than 200,000 men apparently simply did not exist. A larger army on the march lost much of its coherence. Living off the land, it quickly exhausted all available supplies and found itself faced with the choice of achieving a quick victory or beating a hasty retreat.

Civic enthusiasm and military skill were, in combination, capable of raising a mass army and leading it for specific campaigns. But a standing mass army based on universal military training and general mobilization plans could not be maintained on such a narrow base. The permanent nation-in-arms was made possible by a constellation of nineteenth-century technical developments: a revolution in agricultural production that removed the need for the bulk of Europeans to live at the marginal subsistence level;[30] the rise of a processed-food industry; the invention of the telegraph and the steam railway. With these, it became possible to mobilize, supply, and move troops efficiently according to a rational and detailed plan.

The French had discovered the power of ideology. They had created the idea of a military force made up of the nation-in-arms and led by an aristocracy of talent. The legend of revolutionary and Napoleonic armies, a combination of civic élan and military genius, dominated all of Europe. But because ideology and not technology had unleased such forces, the model came to be regarded as too explosive. After 1815, both France and Prussia returned to a more restricted model. The mass armies had not only broadened the political base; they had also encouraged the emergence of a type of officer inclined to define his loyalties in terms of the nation-state rather than of the regime currently in power. The system had not failed, but its implications had not been lost on the leaders of post-Napoleonic Europe. It had worked for revolutions and for Napoleon. Neither was any longer in fashion.

The word "mass" in mid-nineteenth-century Europe had revolutionary connotations. Its entailed social consequences outweighed its military potential. With military service on all levels now regarded as a political role rather than as a social choice, France and Prussia, the two major military powers, were wary of schemes that would put arms into the hands of the general population. [31] Each approached the problem, though, from its own perspective. France, from 1830 to 1870, was governed by what was essentially a middle-class-based regime. The political reliability of the armed forces was conceived as being dependent on excluding aristocrats from the officer corps and keeping the urban workers disarmed. France accordingly maintained an army whose enlisted body comprised long-term rural conscripts and whose officer corps consisted of middle-class careerists. This was backed up by a preponderantly bourgeois National Guard whose membership was based on property qualifications.

In Prussia, the problem was more complicated. The nobility had emerged from the Napoleonic wars with its control of the state largely intact. Thus, drastic measures were taken to reduce the numbers and the prospects of the numerous officers of middle-class origin who had entered the army during the general mobilization of 1813-1815.[32] The relationship between military rank and political power was clearly seen. The period 1819-1860 was one of acrimonious rivalry between the proponents of the regular army, led by Junkers and made up of long-term rural volunteers, and the Landwehr, a militia force with officers drawn from the middle classes.

The middle-class orientation of post-Napoleonic France encouraged a military policy of static conservatism. The nobility was a class small enough in numbers to be ignored safely, while the very numbers of the working class justified a repressive policy. In Prussia, on the other hand, the Junkers were contending with the bourgeoisie, a class especially favored by the economic and social developments of the nineteenth century. Industrialization and urbanization were rapidly increasing the wealth, numbers, and influence of the bourgeoisie. A more ingenious solution was required. The Junkers maintained their control, but at a price. The Landwehr was absorbed into the regular army and in effect abolished. From an autonomous body it was transformed into a general reserve into which citizens passed after a three-year term of training in the regular army.

This administrative transformation had far-reaching political and military consequences. It gave the Junker elite complete control over the military resources of Prussia. However, it also created a regular army whose need for officers exceeded the manpower resources of the nobility. Against all the prejudices of the men who dictated the terms of the solution, the officer corps was opened to large numbers of commoners. Moreover, the sheer size of the new army necessitated the creation of a central administrative and planning body and thus of a bureaucracy functionally independent of the traditional system of upper-class partronage and control.[33] The cumulative effect of these changes made Prussia the foremost continental military power.[34]

The Prussian military reforms of 1859 did more than create a more efficient reserve system and a more professional officer corps. In a sense, the reforms, whose ambiguities will be explored later, erased the implications of class conflict from the concept of the nation-in-arms. General mobilization had previously been an extraordinary summons by the state. The armed forces of the ancien régime had been an extrasocial entity and as such adequate for the quasi-private wars of the preindustrial state. The appeal for popular support was, under these circumstances, a confession of failure. Any kind of broad mobilization was a threat to the nobility's claim to a monopoly of military skills.

The institution of general conscription and regular reserve duty changed all this. It transformed the regular army from the unique military agent to the core of a socially comprehensive system. What had been the privileged defender of the sovereign now become the instrument which trained and administered the military resources of the entire nation-state. General mobilization made what had been a privilege a civic duty. It gave the officer corps the legal authority to draft all the available resorces of the nation into its plan of operation. More significant, it made the conscript and the reserve officer an integral part rather than an emergency adjunct of the military establishment. Professionalism was now judged in terms of ability to utilize nonregular resources rather than operate independently of them. By making military services a general condition, the concept of general mobilization fostered a notion of war as a situation where the interests of the military were also those of the nation.

The immediate consequence of all this was the transformation of the Prussian General Staff into a body fundamentally different in function and outlook from any of its contemporary rivals. Before 1860 the staff function could be roughly described as that of setting up general standards of discipline and training and of devising the tactics and strategy designed to use them most effectively. After 1860, under the guidance of the elder von Moltke, the Prussian army developed a general staff to plan and carry out the process of general mobilization. Previous professional military planning had concerned itself with making the best possible use of the standing army. Under the stimulus of the Prussian military reforms, staff planning became the science of mobilizing the greatest possible number of adequately trained and equipped soldiers and of moving them into position in a swift and coordinated fashion.[35]

The rapid nineteenth century development of railroad and telegraph made this possible. Without it, planned general mobilization would have been no more than a theory. But the decisive factor was the realization that so long as professionals were in complete control there was really no natural antipathy between the nation-in-arms and the regular solider.

An expanded concept of professionalism became the factor which guaranteed the ascendancy of the regular over the citizen-soldier. Conservative governments had avoided universal military training because citizen-soldiers seemed to entail citizen-officers—and this involved giving arms and authority to the very forces they were trying to control. But when the professional officer was given the special role of formulating and executing the plan of general mobilization, the risk was attenuated to the point of becoming negligible. When there were two distinct officer corps, each patently class-based, the matter of control was an obvious source of social and political conflict. But with a single officer corps, structured in terms of responsibility for and involvement with a comprehensive form of public service, such differences were eliminated. Nonregular officers were simply those whose involvement with the plan did not operate on a day-to-day basis.

With the transformation of the officer corps from a class into a bureaucracy, professional training became a process focusing on the acquisition of technical skills. The fact that this process inculcated a particular social attitude[36] could be attributed to the occupational deformation arising from a total dedication to the problems of national security. Everyone under arms now belonged to the same army, but some to a greater degree than others. What had formerly been a threat to the ruling structures became an instrument for extending and refining their apparatus of control.

IV

The Prussian victory of 1870 made Prussia's military system a model to be imitated by every aspiring European national power. Mass armies based on universal military service and directed by a general staff became the fashion. This development had two immediate consequences: a sharp increase in the prestige of the professional officer, and the exaltation and worship of "the plan." The two were interrelated. Universal military training meant that a war would be based on general mobilization, and general mobilization meant that a nation would fight a war according to a timetable which its general staff had worked out in great detail well in advance. It became a dogmatic conviction that without general mobilization the state could not go to war, and that without adherence to the plan, general mobilization could not be carried out. Society, in effect, did not serve the state, it served the plan. The plan defined the political obligations of every citizen.

In more primitive times war had been a contest in skill and

courage between two contending regional but essentially similar elites. The military leaders of France, Prussia, and Austria were in general terms members of a single Europe-wide class. Generals concentrated on their opposite numbers in an effort to prove themselves superior in those qualities held to be the mark of aristocratic distinction. Under the new system the contest shifted into the arena of domestic policy. It was the duty of the professional officer to draw up a program that would result in the most massive and rapid possible thrust of the nation's mobilized resources into the center of enemy resistance. It was the duty of civil authorities to ensure that, once war came, the program would be carried out without delay or hindrance. The actual intentions of the enemy and the play of international forces were of secondary importance. The military had the role of mobilizing the nation's resources to the fullest extent possible, the civilian authorities that of allowing them to do so. Victory was held to be a consequence of the most thorough possible mobilization—an act that unleashed the full power of the nation. Mobilization was The Plan—and the plan, drawn up by the professional staff, was synonymous with the nation-in-arms.

Two incidents at the beginning of World War I dramatized this relationship. In Germany, just prior to the outbreak of hostilities, the emperor was advised that if Germany refrained from an assault on Belgium, Great Britian would remain neutral. He therefore asked the chief of staff if that would be possible. The latter explained that Germany had only one war plan, that of attacking France through Belgium. To attempt to change it now and to shift forces for an attack on Russia would be disastrous. In effect, Germany could not go to war without general mobilization and the mobilization schedules and the strategic plan were by nature inseparable.[37]

Something similar happened in France. Although all available evidence indicated that a massive German thrust would come through Belgium, Joffre persisted in his efforts to mount a French offensive in Alsace-Lorraine. This was the official French strategy; the general mobilization was based on it. As he understood it, the role of the commander was to believe in the plan and to carry it out regardless of circumstances.[38]

The plan was more than a strategic device. It was the articulation of the professional officer's national role. The plan did not simply defend the nation, it was the guarantee of her sovereign existence. It was the plan that made military service a matter of civic responsibility and military leadership the highest form of public service. As the creators and guardians of the plan, the officers were the secular clergy of the nation-state. Theirs was the role of converting society's resources into instruments of the national interest.

The levée en masse had been the consequence of a process which redefined the state in accordance with the demands of society. Society was perceived as possessing energies and capacities the state lacked. These energies and capacities, however, proved so explosive that it was recognized that they could be unleashed only in the greatest emergency and must be restrained at all other times.

Universal military service and general mobilization did just the reverse. Society was redefined in accordance with the demands of the state. In contrast to the leaders of the ancien régime, who had an obsessive distrust of class differences and private interests, the proponents of the new nationalism regarded them as malleable assets. Class identity was secondary to the national interest and private concerns elevated by their absorption into the plans of national mobilization. Working-class organizations could be a source of mass support; large-scale industrial enterprises became indispensable purveyors to national security. There were thus no cautionary limits to national military service.

The transformation was to a large extent ideological. On the continent, nationalism replaced liberalism as the enlightened creed and reversed perception of the state-society relationship. For the liberals, society was prior to the state in both historical and normative terms. For the nationalists, it was the other way around.

The leaders of the French Revolution had regarded the nobility as corrupt and enervated largely because it had, in its identification with the state, withdrawn itself from direct contact with society. The nationalism of the nineteenth century considered the civil service and the army to be progressive forces, the backbone of the political system. Without them, society was incapable of undertaking large-scale and therefore ennobling enterprises.

The extension of civil rights had been feared lest it bring with it claims for a greater share of ruling-class privileges. Now it was discovered that a sufficiently large number of the newly enfranchised were content with the opportunity of wearing the uniform of national service. Previously a concept which justified a higher degree of political participation, the mass army was transformed into an institution which justified the privilege and powers of a narrow elite. Its energies were subordinated to the will of a particular structure of authority and dedicated to the maintenance of a special class.

The realization that military professionalization offered a career independent of conventional social and political norms opened the way to the creation of a more representative officer corps. The structure of military rank and privilege became for the first time a self-regulating social system. Changes and fluctuations within the military took place in virtual isolation from the structure of domestic politics. Secure in this knowledge, the military profession could recruit and train members on its own terms. The officer corps changed its social composition, becoming a much more heterogeneous body whose membership was determined by the logic of its bureaucratic requirements. In Prussia, for example, the proportion of officers with noble to those with middle-class origins changed from 65-35 in 1860 to 30-70 in 1913, and in the higher ranks, namely, generals and colonels, from 86-14 to 52-48. In absolute terms the number of lieutenants of noble origin fell by three hundred in the period between 1873 and 1913. This reflected not so much an increase in egalitarian outlook among the Junkers as the personnel demands of a mass army. By 1927, in the purely volunteer and numerically restricted Reichswehr, ideological reliability was again a factor, and the proportion of officers of noble origin had risen to 54 per cent.[39] In France something similar occurred, though from an opposite direction. Members of the French nobility, who ever since the Revolution had been regarded with suspicion by Republicans, Orleanists, and Bonapartists, and who had held themselves aloof from their traditional military calling, began, with the institution of mass military service in the closing days of the Second Empire, to enter the officer corps in increasing numbers.[40]

The conclusion seems obvious. Where universal military service is accepted, members of the profession do not feel that dissidence among themselves represents a threat. In any event, the autonomy such an armed force gives to the officer corps enables it to screen and indoctrinate its members effectively. An army of volunteer careerists is, on the other hand, a self-segregating body. The insurance of loyalty becomes, therefore, an explicit criterion of officer recruitment.

Universal military service thus had the effect of broadening the class origins of the professional officer corps. Its adoption brought about more middle-class representation in an increasing middle-class Germany and increased aristocratic representation in a nationalistically revived France. Similar tendencies can be observed even in the absence of a national military tradition. In the United States, for example, the establishment after World War II of the first peacetime system of universal military service seems to have resulted in a broad extension of the social basis of officer recruitment. During the period 1933-1950, the proportion of officers with upper- and upper-middle-class backgrounds to those with lower-class origins changed from 76-24 to 50-50.[41] It remains to be seen whether the reestablishment of an American volunteer army will have the same effect on the officer corps as it did in the Weimar Republic, i.e., a narrowing of the social base and an increased stress on the traditional function of political loyalty.

Broadening the social base does not necessarily result in a more popularly responsive officer corps. Under the old system with an officer corps whose members preponderantly were of noble origin, the primary loyalty of military leaders had been to their class, an entity which they identified with the state. In an essentially classless officer corps, the emphasis shifted. The primary allegiance of the military professional was transferred to the corporate body of which he was a member.[42] This body and not his class origins was the primary source of the status and authority he enjoyed. Under the old system, those officers whose professional status was regarded as based on the possession of certain objective skills, e.g., artillerymen or engineers, were a marginal group with low status and limited prospects. The true officer was known by his pedigree. The new system institutionalized professional criteria. Status was determined not by origins but by the process of formation. The inner elite was henceforth to be made up of those whose military experience conformed most closely to the professional ideal, i.e., those who had gone to the academy, been to the staff college, had the proper staff assignments, and so on.

The military process of education and assignment served to advance those whose professional experience continually strengthened their sense of identification with their professional roles. Officers acheived status not because they were already members of the ruling class, i.e., the administrative apparatus of the state, or because they offered it special skills, but because they met the specifications of the corporate body of professional soldiers. These specifications were determined in the context of universal military training and the plans for mass mobilization. The universal scope of military responsibility created the sense of a class-free, self-determining role.[43]

V

Before the French Revolution, the social group that ruled the country and conducted its diplomacy in effect also waged its wars. By the end of the nineteenth century this was no longer the case. Internal politics, international relations, and the conduct of war had come to represent three separate and self-contained fields. A common interest in maintaining the established order bound their practitioners together, but socially and administratively they functioned quite apart. The officer corps represented the most extreme development in a trend that could also be observed in the diplomatic corps and in the administrative bureaucracy. The officer corps had become a truly professional body, self-contained and in most respects answerable only to itself. In this context, the outbreak of World War I represented a shift in power. Military affairs assumed absolute preeminence. The conventional system of international relations was suspended and the internal political process dampened.

According to the contemporary descriptions, the populations of the Western parliamentary governments obeyed the mobilization schedules not merely without any notable dissent but with wild enthusiasm. To all classes, military service appeared to offer a level of social-political participation more vivid and satisfactory than that provided by conventional social and economic experience. The civilian leaders of that period, whatever their persuasion, offered no opposition to the generals. The most antinationalist of them, the leaders of the Socialist International, either lost all influence over their followers or joined in the general clamor for all-out war.

Responsibility for conducting the war passed almost immediately from civilian to military hands. The conventional apparatus of government in France and Germany seemed to fall into the role of accepting military estimates of manpower and material requirements and organizing the nonmobilized population to acheive them. The moderate exceptions to this were Great Britian, which had gone into the war without a general mobilization system, and Russia, where pre-nineteenth-century military conventions still prevailed.

The professional monopoly of military leadership and strategic direction did not, however, lead to a more inspired and rational level of warfare. World War I was the most complete conceivable test of a formal military system. The planning and conduct of operations were almost exclusively in the hands of career officers recruited, trained, and assigned within a corporate body that had for about forty years planned and prepared itself for exactly this eventuality. From beginning to end in that war, little was improvised. Every notable action was the product of massive and detailed planning.[44] The results were almost uniformly horrendous.

In one sense, professionalism had triumphed. The general staffs were able to mobilize more men, engage in a more intensive level of combat, and sustain it over a longer span of time than ever before. In the political sense of being able to mobilize the resources of society in pursuit of the national interest, professionalism was demonstrably successful. In the military sense of producing results commensurate with the expenditure of resources involved, professionalism has clearly failed.

The military policy of all the major powers involved had been based on the expectation of a decisive victory achieved through the full execution of the plan. The mobilized army was the nation-in-arms. According to the nationalist dogma, this was bound to be a morally and materially superior force. When the plan collapsed, the result was a physical and intellectual deadlock. The professional reflex was to fall back into the area where their special skills had been patently effective, to mobilize yet more men, and to demand a greater share of society's material resources. If a strategic doctrine can be said to have emerged from World War I, it can be formulated as the belief that the losing side was the one whose society first admitted that it no longer had the energy or resources to carry on the struggle. Defeat, as the Germany army discovered in 1919, was not physical and did not occur on the battlefield. It was a form of spiritual betrayal emanating from somewhere in the rear. Something or someone had kept the nation from committing itself fully to the struggle.

Each side was afterward confronted with the incontrovertible fact that the grand plan had failed. Much time was spent between the world wars examining and seeking to draw lessons from that discovery. The result, however, was not to abandon planning but to reformulate its nature and scope. The general conclusion seems to have been that grand plans were undesirable because they were too massive, complicated, costly, and inflexible. The specific conclusions drawn differed. The French decided that they would stick to general mobilization and do without a strategic plan. They would wait behind the Maginot Line and see what the Germans would do. The Germans decided to forgo a grand strategy in favor of a series of limited ad hoc operations.

Politically, the great change was in the realization that general mobilization did not simply militarize the state. Rather, it made both state and society active parts of the military effort. The idea that wars are as apt to be lost behind the lines as on the battlefields had become a dogma. In contrast to World War I, when civilian leaders had immediately stepped aside and military operations became paramount, the mobilization of the domestic economy and the maintenance of domestic morale were treated as an integral part of the war effort. War had come to imply not only inspired leadership of the forces in combat but a similar effort in every other aspect of national life. Mobilization on an ideological basis gained ascendency over mobilization on the basis of military plans. For this last role, military leaders were professionally unprepared.

National leadership and military leadership were united. In the nations engaged in World War II, political executives took on the active roles of commanders in cheif of the armed forces and the charismatic posture of social prophets. They promised not only victory but their society's transition thereby to a more elevated level. As in the time of the French Revolution, military mobilization was justified not only in terms of the national interest but almost equally as strongly on the grounds of social change. The demands of total mobilization had apparently led the mass army into precisely those policies it has been designed to avoid

VI

Among societies functioning at the advanced industrial level, mass armies appear to be vanishing. Their social costs are increasingly regarded as being too high, their political consequences as insufficiently subject to popular control. Mass armies are seen more and more as involving levels of public expenditure, demands for personal sacrifice, distributions of personal income and privilege, and commitments to foreign policies that fit neither the needs nor the interests of society. The status of the professional officer has also changed. The professional soldier in the context of the mass army is no longer generally perceived as the highest form of public servant, the one most directly concerned with the national interest. Rather, he is one among a multitude of public careerists. The fact that he belongs to a group which is the most autonomous and tightly organized of all does not make him a qualitatively different kind of servant but, rather, one who emphasizes the general bureaucratic problems of public responsibility.[45]

Technical military developments have contributed to this. The increasing dependence on highly complex systems of mass destruction has placed the idea of national security in an ambiguous context. Technical developments have also raised the question of whether the military—or any other profession, for that matter—has the moral and political qualities appropriate to the area it controls. The existence of ultimate weapons has made it difficult to place military operations in a rational context.

At the level of conventional wars, the overall contribution of professional leadership has become subject to doubt. Professionally led armies have not resulted in war's becoming a more humane or economical instrument of national policy. The general record in the twentieth century has not been an encouraging one. Under professional direction, wars have become bloodier, longer, and less amenable to moderating limits.

Parallel social developments may also be undermining the viability of the professionally led mass army. There are general indications among the societies of the advanced industrialized world that the nation-state is losing its appeal as the preponderant source of social affiliation. Regional, occupational, class, and ethnic attributes are acquiring greater weight. The social attractiveness of military service seems to have almost entirely disappeared. The political attractiveness of the mass army has, as a result, greatly declined. It has become an agent of strain rather than one of control.

The professionally directed mass army functioned, as I have argued, as an agency which could sponsor a higher degree of political participation without imposing an equivalent degree of social change. It could thereby increase the effectiveness of the political apparatus without stimulating any significant transformation of the encompassed social structure. This was possible as long as the national military effort operated entirely within the context of a professionally controlled plan.

The nineteenth-century Industrial Revolution created an awesome technological apparatus. Universal military service was a novel method for demonstrating to society the tremendous resources the state had at its disposal and of giving members a concrete and controlled sense of participation in this power.

Military service was accordingly more popular among citizens of rural than of urban origins, less resisted by the poor than by the rich, and more acceptable to the disenfranchised than to the politically active.[46] For this reason, too, perhaps, the air force was the most popular and glamorous of the services. As master of the technological ritual and custodian of its secrets, the professional soldier acquired tremendous prestige.

This system broke down at two points: first, when the general mobilization plan ceased to be synonymous with decisive victory; and second, when the state took on an independent role in the mobilization of social resources and provided alternative modes of social and political participation. The development of consumer technology and the consequent rising expectations have contributed to this latter effect. To the degree that a society is industrialized, its members are active possessors of its advanced products and active clients for its sophisticated services. When military service came to mean giving up one's own auto rather than acquiring the opportunity to drive one, being tied to a particular place rather than being given the chance to leave home, deferring one's education rather than gaining the opportunity to acquire one, the popularity of military service was bound to decline.

If the factors of social and political mobilization and technological control have a diminishing association with the professional military establishments of the advanced industrialized societies, there are some states where they are still attrative. This is the case with the members of the Soviet bloc and of countries, such as Turkey, Israel, and Algeria, where armed conflict helped to create and sustain a new sense of national identity. But all of these, with the notable exceptions of Turkey and the Soviet Union, are national regimes which came into being after World War II. It can be argued that they represent a repetition of nineteenth-century European developments. These are states where national military service is equated with the ideological basis for political independence. Their reliance on the mass army may very well be an integral part of their political systems.

In those societies which are now in the process of abandoning the mass army, the position of the professional soldier is becoming much more problematic. Societies of this type are invariably dependent on a highly advanced technology. The substitution of a volunteer force must, for the reasons already presented, coincide with a decline in the status and prestige of the officer corps. We are thus presented with the prospect of armed forces whose technological requirements are higher and growing increasingly more complex, and of an officer corps whose career attractiveness is in a process of continual diminution. The resolution of this dilemma, like the forces which created it, may well involve processes and changes that go far beyond the military sphere.

NOTES

1. Niccolo Machiavelli, *The Art of War,* trans. Ellis Farneworth, rev., with an introduction by Neal Wood (Indianapolis: Bobbs-Merrill, 1965), pp. 7 ff.
2. Max Weber, "The Origins of Discipline in War," in *Economy and Society,* 3 vols., ed. G. Roth and C. Wittich (Totowa, N.J.: Bedminster Press, 1968), 3: 1150 ff.
3. Joseph R. Strayer, *On the Medieval Origins of the Modern State* (Princeton, N.J.: Princeton University Press, 1970), pp. 24ff.
4. *The Military Balance: 1967-68* (London: Institute for Strategic Studies, 1968). The respective figures are 264,000, 325,000, and 340,000.
5. Gustav Roloff, "Moritz von Oranien und die Begründung des modernen Heeres," Preussische Jahrbuch 3: (1903) 255-276, esp. pp. 264 ff.
6. Charles Wilson, *The Dutch Republic and the Civilization of the Seventeenth Century* (New York: McGraw-Hill, 1968), pp. 8 ff. Also Gordon Griffith, "The Revolutionary Character of the Revolt of the Netherlands," Comparative Studies in History and Society 2: (1960) 452-472.
7. Aquinas, *Selected Political Writings,* ed. A. P. D'Entreves (New York: Macmillan, 1959), pp. 159-160.
8. Jan Den Tex, *Oldenbarnevelt,* trans. R. P. Powell, 2 vols. (Cambridge, England, at the University Press 1973), 1: 85 ff. The revolt began in 1566. It was not until 1586, after repeated attempts to obtain a conventional sovereign from France or England, that the Dutch took political leadership into their own hands.
9. Robert P. Adams, *The Better Part of Valor: More, Erasmus, Colet, and Vives, on Humanism, War and Peace, 1496-1535* (Seattle: University of Washington Press, 1962), pp. 100 ff.
10. Gerhard Oestreich, "Justus Lipsius als Theoretiker des neuzeitlichen Machtstaates," Historische Zeitschrift 82: (1956) 31-78. Reprinted in *Geist und Gestalt des frühmodernen Staates* (Berlin: Dunker und Humblot 1969), pp. 35-79.
11. Geist und Gestalt, p. 37 ff.
12. Werner Hahlweg, *Die Heeresreform der Oranier und die Antike* (Berlin: Junker und Dünnhaupt 1941), passim. Also Michael Roberts, "The Military Revolution, 1560-1650," in *Essays in Swedish History* (Minneapolis: University of Minnesota Press, 1967), pp. 196 ff.

13. Jan Willem Wijn, *Het Krijgswezen in Tijd van Prins Maurits* (Utrecht: Drukkerij 1934), pp. 546 ff., Hoeijenbos & Co.
14. Friedrich Meinecke, "The Century of Universal Military Service," in *The Warfare of a Nation,* trans. J. A. Spaulding (Worcester, Mass.: 1915), pp. 47-52.
15. Nuria Sales de Bohigas, "Some Opinions on Exemption from Military Service in Nineteenth-Century Europe," Comparative Studies in History and Society 10 (1967-1968): 261-289.
16. Robert Southey, *Letters from England,* ed. J. Simmons (London, Cresset Press, 1951), p. 93. The telegraph of this reference is a semaphore, not electric.
17. Theodore Roosevelt, "Universal service and universal suffrage go hand in hand," and Tocqueville and Taine, "L'obligation militaire est la contrepartie et comme la rançon du droit politique," are both quoted in Sales de Bohigas, "Some Opinions," p. 262.
18. L. Hartman, *Les Officiers de l'armée royale et la Révolution* (Paris: F. Alcan 1910), p. 13.
19. Karl Demeter, *The German Officer Corps* (New York: Praeger 1965), pp. 18 ff.
20. C. Woodham-Smith, *The Reason Why* (New York: Dutton, 1954), passim.
21. P. Heisieck, ed., *Rayonnement de Lyautey* (Paris: Gallimard, 1947), pp. 119-200.
22. Emmanuel Joseph Sieyès, *What is the Third Estate?*trans. M. Blondel (New York, Prager 1965), pp. 53-58.
23. Ibid., pp. 59 ff.
24. François Furet and Denis Richet, *The French Revolution* (New York: Macmillan, 1969), p. 116.
25. John Ellis, *Armies in Revolution* (New York Oxford University Press 1974), pp. 79 ff.
26. Ibid., pp. 88 ff.
27. Roberts, "Military Revolution," pp. 209 ff.; Demeter, *German Officer Corps,* p. 19.
28. Hartmann, *Officers,* pp. 30-35.
29. David G. Chandler, *The Campaigns of Napoleon* (New York: Macmillan, 1966), p. xii.
30. Jean Fourastié, *The Causes of Wealth,* trans. and ed. T. Caplow (New York: Free Press, 1960), pp. 75 ff.
31. Raoul Girardet, *La Société militaire dans la France contemporaine (1815-1939)* (Paris Plon 1953), pp. 55 ff.; Gordon Craig, *The Politics of the Prussian Army 1640-1945* (New York: Oxford University Press, 1956), p. 74.
32. Demeter, *German Officer Corps,* pp. 17 ff.
33. Craig, *Politics,* pp. 194-197. "A division commander receiving orders from Moltke at Königgratz is reported to have said, 'This is all very well, but who is General Moltke?'" (p. 197).
34. Ibid., pp. 139 ff.
35. Michael Howard, *The Franco-Prussian War* (London: Collier, 1961), pp. 24 ff.
36. Bengt Abrahamson, *Military Professionalization and Political Power* (Beverly Hills, Calif.: Sage, 1972), pp. 59 ff.
37. Craig, *Politics.* See also Gerhard Ritter, *The Schlieffen Plan,* trans. A. and E. Wilson (London: O. Wolff 1958), passim.
38. Barbara Tuchman, *The Guns of August* (New York: Macmillan, 1962), pp. 182 ff.
39. Demeter, *German Officer Corps,* pp. 24, 54.
40. Girardet, *Société militaire,* pp. 186 ff.
41. Morris Janowitz, *The Professional Soldier* (Glencoe, Ill.: Free Press, 1960), p. 90.
42. Abrahamson, *Military Professionalization,* pp. 120 ff.

43. S. P. Huntington, *The Soldier and the State* (Cambridge: Harvard University Press, 1957), pp. 14 ff.
44. The German operations on the Eastern Front were an exception to this rule. There were no pre-1914 plans for them.
45. Abrahamson, *Military Professionalization,* passim.
46. Sales de Bohigas, "Some Opinions," p. 263.

Chapter 7

MIDDLE-CLASS SOCIETY

AND THE RISE OF MILITARY PROFESSIONALISM:

THE DUTCH ARMY 1589-1609

I

Two factors characterize the emergence of the modern armed force: the substitution of technical proficiency for personal prowess; and the transformation of military operations from a self-liquidating form of venture capitalism into a systematically budgeted branch of public administration. The first, the main subject of this essay, has involved the creation of objective standards for training and commanding fighting men. The second has entailed abandoning the notion of war as an activity the value of whose immediate conquests was expected to equal or surpass its costs. Both these changes have been critical in the breakdown of feudalism and the construction of the modern state.

The importance of these factors is well known. However, the fact that the decisive steps in institutionalizing them were first taken in the northern Netherlands at the time of its successful revolt against Spain merits further investigation. The first modern army and the earliest rationalized forms of military administration

Reprinted from the journal Armed Forces and Society, *Volume I, No. 4 (Summer 1975).*

were created not in the major powers of the time but in a relatively backward and decidedly unmilitary society. The unanticipated character of this raises broader questions about the nature of social and political innovations and the role that armed forces play in them.

The seventeenth-century Dutch Republic is one of the anomalies of modern European history. In an age of absolute monarchs, its government had no clearly defined center of power. In a time of aristocratic preponderence, its society was dominated by a class of merchant oligarchs. Most surprising of all, this nonaristocratic, loosely governed state created an army that was a model for its neighbors and the school for a generation of European commanders.

These achievements did not pass unnoticed. The political and economic literature of the seventeenth century abounds in references to "the miracle of the Dutch Republic."[1] But "miracle" is the key word. True, Dutch commercial and economic activities were the most advanced in Europe. To be sure, the Dutch enjoyed an unparalleled degree of personal freedom and their nation was a byword for political and religious tolerance. There is no doubt that the technology and the schools of natural and physical science and classical philology of the northern Neitherlands were universally resorted to. All these were aspects of a miracle. The achievements of the Dutch defied conventional expectations. Wonder at them has persisted to modern times. "States have flourished," it has recently been written, "which meet none of the criteria of the political scientist, for example, the Netherlands in the seventeenth century."[2]

It does, nevertheless, strain the imagination to believe that a chain of worldly successes like this were accomplished accidentally. "Les quoiques," as Proust has somewhere remarked, "sont toujours les parceques méconnus." The Dutch, for one thing, were too notoriously calculating for the totality of their achievement to be written off as something adventitious. Political, religious, and economic decisions in the United Provinces of the Netherlands, the official name of the Dutch Republic, were more widely and openly debated than anywhere else in seventeenth-century Europe.[3] Few, if any, of the basic Dutch policies were the result of an arbitrary decision by a single individual. To a greater degree than those of perhaps any other nation-state of the time, seventeenth-century Dutch institutions reflect the outlook and preoccupations of a particular class, the urban bourgeoisie of Amsterdam and its neighboring cities.[4]

Conventional explanations of notable success in the political and especially in the military spheres have a tendency to find its origins in the existence of a strong centralized government or in the active stimulus of some national tradition. The government of the Dutch Republic was, however, the reverse of centralized. As Sir William Temple, one of its more acute contemporary observers, remarked: ". . . It cannot properly be stiled a commonwealth, but is rather a Confederacy of Seven Sovereign Provinces united together for their common and mutual defense, without any dependence one upon the other."[5]

In military matters, the situation was even more striking. The Dutch army was perhaps the most efficient and certainly the most widely imitated force of its time. But it was composed largely of mercenaries. A national military tradition was almost entirely absent; and the dominant social and political class—the urban merchant oligarchs—had a positive aversion to military careers in any form. As Huizinga noted, "It was only rarely that the Dutch themselves bore arms against the enemy. They suffered rather than waged the war; fighting was left largely to troops recruited abroad."[6]

This unique combination of middle-class ascendency, political decentralization, and military proficiency is the subject of this essay. The combination was, to be sure, an unstable one. It held together roughly from 1590 to 1670. After that it began, for reasons outside the scope of this paper, to fall apart. By the eighteenth century the Dutch Republic was a second- or third-order European power. For eighty years, however, the Dutch competed as an equal with European states with far larger populations and greater internal resources.

More specifically, this essay will examine the relationship between Dutch political and social composition and the creation of the first modern professional army. The Dutch were the first nation to impose rationalized patterns of performance on their troops and also the first to guide military operations by what would now be called criteria of civilian control. That they did so in the absence of a strong political system and without the assistance of an indigenous military caste makes their achievement all the more noteworthy.

II

> Concord's true picture shineth in this art,
> Where divers men and women rankèd be,
> And every one doth dance a several part,
> Yet all as one in measure do agree,
> Observing perfect uniformity:
> All turn together, all together trace,
> And all together honour and embrace.[7]

The reform and professionalization of the Dutch army are principally associated with the name of Maurice of Nassau (1567-1625), the second son of William the Silent (1533-1584). In his own right—as a commander, as the son of the man regarded as the embodiment of the revolt against Spain, and as the actual head of the most important family in the Netherlands—Maurice was an imposing figure. But it would be a mistake to regard the military changes as being purely his own invention. In matters of strategy and overall organization, he worked in close collaboration and perhaps even followed the direction of the civilian head of the Dutch Republic, Johan van Oldenbarnevelt (1547-1619). In matters of tactical reform and organization, he seems to have shared the responsibility equally with his cousin, William Louis of Nassau (1560-1620).[8]

Be that as it may, the changes instituted in the Dutch armed forces corresponded strikingly with the outlook expected of a middle-class society. In conformity with the middle-class Calvinist outlook, which spurned the notion of a hierarchically organized society, Dutch society was organized on a pluralistic basis.[9] There was, in practice, a clear-cut division between civil and military branches. The commander of the armed force was purely a military leader. The States General, the national parliament, gave him his orders and supervised their execution through the commissarlike agency of field deputies.[10] The conduct of war was thus continually subject to bourgeois precepts of sound management.

The immediate effects of this were twofold. The size of the army was brought into line with the resources of the state. The fiscal system was organized to place military financing on a firm footing. Soldiers could expect year-round employment and regularly paid wages.[11] The terms of service were no longer tied to the duration of a particular campaign but, rather, to the upkeep of a standing army.

This in itself would have been enough to change the nature of war. The Spanish, English, and aristocratic Dutch armies which had, up to that time, contested the control of the northern Netherlands, invariably had seen their plans founder because of morale. When arrears in pay rose beyond a certain point, as they almost always did, the soldiers would mutiny and refuse to fight. Worst of all, victories in the field were constantly cut short as soldiers went on strike for compensation for their success or else indulged in orgies of looting in conquered areas.[12]

The aristocratic concept of war as the most proper occupation for gentlemen promoted this state of affairs. Upper-class traditions fostered the notion that a soldier fought for glory and from a sense of duty to his sovereign.[13] His reward was the gratitude of his ruler and the property of his enemies. Ransom and plunder were considered the proper remuneration of valor.[14] Soldiers were expected, as gentlemen of fortune, to accept them in lieu of deferred pay. Rulers begrudged expenditures on an organization whose effectiveness was measured by the degree to which it was self-supporting.

The weakness of this doctrine, the notorious *bellum se ipsum alet* (war should feed on itself), was that it was suitable only for marauding expeditions. It destroyed that upon which it fed. The Netherlands was both the wealthiest province of the Spanish empire and the home base of the Dutch revolt. Both sides depended on the financial resources of the Netherlands to support their military efforts. But the Spanish, burdened by the hidalgo tradition, were powerless to make use of these resources. "It was not the prince of Orange [i.e., William the Silent] who had lost the Low Countries," said their governor general, "but the soldiers born in Valladolid and Toledo, because the mutineers had driven money out of Antwerp and destroyed all credit."[15]

A society such as the Dutch Republic, dominated by a merchant class, had no such problems. The maintenance of commerce and credit was accepted as a worthwhile end in itself. Investment in an armed force was regarded as one of the fixed expenditures of that trading company in extended form, the Dutch city. Commerce, not war, was the major occupation of the state and of its rulers. In marked contrast with the Spanish, the Dutch strategy was guided by its economic base.

The reduction of Dutch forces to a size consonant with the state's financial resources laid the groundwork for a series of radical military reforms.[16] By placing the soldiers on a salaried basis, the Dutch transformed the army's social outlook. The organization was to be held together, not by its sense of honor and loyalty to its sovereign, but by the terms of contracts. The root of its discipline was no longer an inner code but the objectively verifiable standard of regular work for regular pay. Its members were brought into line by a materialistic standard that determined the value of their services. Regular pay destroyed the aristocratic ethos. The salaried worker was not a gentleman.

These changes transformed the mercenary composition of the Dutch forces from a source of weakness to a pillar of strength. Wages regularly paid were a stronger inducement to faithful service than honor intermittently satisfied. The regularity of pay also systemized the concept of military duties. A chronically unpaid army was difficult to control in the field. Disciplining it in the lulls between fighting was virtually out of the question, particularly when its members had a sense of unrequited duty. An army on a secure financial footing was, on the other hand, at all times accountable to its commanders. The periods between campaigns could be systematically employed to improve its organization and its skills.

The advantages of this newfound control are depicted in a book of engravings, published in 1607, *the Wapenhandelinghe* (The

Exercise of Arms) by Jacob de Gheyn.[17] This work consists of a series of 116 plates—42 for the caliver (or arquebus, a light firearm used without a fork), 42 for the musket, and 32 for the pike. The engravings illustrate, in serial order, the postures and movements involved in the use of these three basic infantry weapons. In their entirety, they constitute a striking early use of a book as an instrument of practical instruction.

The *Wapenhandelinghe* is one of the earliest manuals of arms. It was obviously influenced by the numerous fencing books printed throughout Europe after about 1530.[18] The importance and novelty of de Gheyn's work lie in the systematic arrangement of its plates and the comprehensiveness of the accompanying text. The illustrations and their descriptions were arranged to form an integrated instructional device, perhaps the first ever printed. Four unique features were combined to achieve this: (1) the use of a given weapon is broken down into a series of distinct component steps; (2) these steps are arranged in a numbered, logical order; (3) an explicit verbal command is attached to each step; and (4) the series of steps and commands form a full cycle.

The *Wapenhandelinghe* manifests the intellectual and social revolution effected by the development of mechanically printed and illustrated books. These brought about a transformation of knowledge through their use of what William Ivins has called "exactly repeatable statements."[19] A technique or a natural observation could, by this method, be fixed in a form that accurately and verifiably conveyed its author's intention. Operations were described in a manner that any reasonably literate person could understand. The faithful transmission of knowledge and its systematic development were thus made possible.

Printed illustrated books found an almost immediate market as popular instruments of systematic instruction.[20] Fencing, in particular, was a popular subject. A series of illustrated manuals established the various postures and movements of the art.[21] De Gheyn's book went beyond this. The illustrated concepts of serial order, appended verbal commands, and full cycle were not merely instructional but also testing devices. This combination served both pupil and instructor. The application of what was being taught could be immediately demonstrated and evaluated. In the

Wapenhandelinghe we have the first verifiable system of mass indoctrination and control.[22]

Troops carefully drilled in the depicted techniques were not only able accurately to repeat every one of the steps—this in itself no mean feat—but in doing so also became an instrument which could, so to speak, be programmed. The acts that had been carefully fixed into the repertory of the soldier could be produced by specific commands. The role of the soldier was now defined by his ability to respond with precision to the instructions of his supervisors. Both the competence and the rate of productivity of every individual in the system could be systematically controlled and objectively evaluated. By the same token, the competence and productivity of a junior officer or NCO could be measured according to his ability to manipulate a file of soldiers in a uniform and rapid execution of these steps.

This technology was made massively applicable by yet another intellectual factor, the revival of interest in classical antiquity. From Roman and Byzantine military treatises, the Dutch revived the legionary concept of fixed and ordered formations. Since the beginning of the sixteenth century this concept had been in the air. But the Dutch were the first to combine the notion of a fixed military order with the use of firearms. In particular, they adopted a maneuver called the *countermarch* to implement their serial analysis of the successive steps involved in the use of weapons.[23]

The idea of the countermarch is simple enough: it is a maneuver whereby the front rank of a formation turns and marches to the rear. Joined to the *Wapenhandelinghe,* however, it transformed a body of men equipped with firearms into a unit of continuous production. The tactical operation was as follows: soldiers would be ordered into ranks, approximately five deep. The first rank would fire and march to the rear, where it would begin to reload. While engaged in this process, it would advance successively as other ranks fired and executed the countermarch. It would then reemerge as the front rank, with its cycle fully completed, ready to fire again.

The Dutch army thus appears to have been the first social system where technique and control were systematically united. A practical operation was organized so that its execution was also its proof.[24] The competence of troops and leaders was thus subject to mechanical and quantitative criteria. The variable of continuous firepower was made a function of a fixed relationship between the individual's use of his assigned tool and the commander's control of his company. An unprecedented degree of exactitude and regularity was established in the use of both weapons and commands. A numerical cast of mind became a requisite of military expertise.

De Gheyn's work does not merely represent an artist's observations..It is, in fact, the statement of a practicing soldier. There is conclusive evidence that it was conceived and commissioned in 1596 by Johann II of Nassau (1561-1623), the cousin of Maurice and the younger brother of his close collaborator, William Louis.[25] The book was designed to be a manual of instruction for the Dutch armed forces. In succeeding years, it went through several editions and was translated and adapted for use in France, Germany, and England.

The interest of Johann of Nassau in the systematic education of soldiers is well attested. He is credited with establishing—in 1619 at Siegen, in Western Germany—the first modern military academy, a school designed to give military instruction to the sons of the German Protestant nobility, with a syllabus based largely on Greek and Roman histories and military works. The concept of the school was in all probability his, but it is clear that the content of its curriculum was borrowed from the approach and practices of the Dutch army. In particular, he drew heavily on the studies, innovations, and experience of his brother William Louis, the deputy commander of the Dutch army.[26]

The three cousins were remarkable in their time for being military commanders with university backgrounds. Johann and William Louis had attended the University of Heidelberg; Maurice had studied at Leiden. As a result or by coincidence, all three were known for the importance they attached to the military utility of formal knowledge. Johann and William Louis drew on Greek and Roman sources as models of military discipline and organization. William Louis had a scholar on his staff whose special assignment was to select and translate pertinent passages from classical authors. Maurice was a pioneer in applying mathematics in rationalizing military formations and operations. Simon Stevin (1548-1620), the great Dutch mathematician, was a high-ranking member of his staff.[27]

Earlier application of Roman military procedure had stressed the use of regular formations and ordered maneuvers. The Dutch, however, took a step forward. They emphasized the importance not so much of discipline as of command. The use of verbal orders as a tactical device was a major preoccupation of William Louis. This concept was directly borrowed from the late Roman military treatises of Leo the Emperor and Aelian Tacticus.[28] From Leo, in particular, William Louis derived the radical idea that soldiers should remain silent in the ranks. His suggestions were adopted by Maurice. In 1597 the words of command for drill were established in definitive form for the five languages most commonly used in the Dutch army: Dutch, German, French, English, and Scottish. [29]

The drastic improvement in command and control effected by these innovations also made possible a series of extensive reforms in the Dutch army's tactical organization. The size of basic units was reduced from 3,000 to 135 men. The equipment of the soldiers was standardized. The ratio of firearms to pikes drastically changed in favor of the former. The number of officers and NCOs were sharply increased.

A comparison with the Spanish tercio, its major adversary and at that time the most effective European fighting unit, illustrates the extent of the Dutch innovations. The tercio was an infantry body of roughly twelve companies, designed to operate as a cohesive group. The companies were supportive, not self-sustaining. Each was equipped preponderantly with either pikes or firearms, with one company of firearms to every five of pikes. A pike company had 11 officers, 219 pikemen, and 20 musketeers. A firearm company had 11 officers and 239 men equipped with firearms.[30]

The basic Dutch company had, on the other hand, 135 men: 13 officers and NCOs, 45 pikemen, 74 equipped with firearms, and 3 pages.[31] It was designed to be a complete tactical entity. If these companies were aggregated in approximately similar groups, six Spanish companies and eleven Dutch, the Dutch total of 1,485 would comprise 143 officers, 33 pages, 495 pikemen, and 814 men with firearms. The Spanish total of 1,500 would, on the other hand, comprise 66 officers, 1,095 pikemen, and 339 men with firearms. The Dutch thus would have a superiority of more than two to one in officers, two-and-one-half to one in firearms.[32] Furthermore, if the number of firearms is broken down into light pieces, i.e., calivers and arquebuses, and heavy ones, i.e., muskets, the Dutch would have 330 muskets and 484 calivers, and the Spanish 115 muskets and 224 arquebuses. In heavy firearms, the Dutch would thus have an advantage of almost three to one.

The Dutch emphasis on firepower can, however, be misleading. If wage scales are any indication, the pike was still regarded as the predominant, or at any rate the most valued, weapon. The wages of pikemen were on the average 20 per cent higher than those of soldiers equipped with firearms. Maurice's earliest military experiments were conducted entirely with pikemen and swordsmen. His decision to concentrate on firearms was based on organizational and logistical, not tactical, grounds.[33] It was the value of the system itself rather than that of its component tools that determined his choice.

Firearms replaced pikes for much the same reason they had replaced the crossbow and the longbow. Firearms economized on training and minimized individual skill and experience. It took years to produce a competent archer and perhaps a generation to form a cohesive mass of pikemen. A body of musketeers could, with the proper methods, be drilled into proficiency in a matter of months. The very inaccuracy and unreliability of firearms relegated individual military prowess to minor importance. The vital elements were the development of a mechanical standard of performance and the inculcation of habits of obedience. The Dutch method employed firearms as a part of the equipment of the system and not as *individual* weapons. The achievement of a mass effect thus became a matter of technique and not of morale. Opposing systems were dependent on heroic leadership and social solidarity; the Dutch relied on regular wages and mechanical controls.

This reform of warfare was analogous to the change, in industrial production, from a craft to an assembly line mode. It eliminated the need for highly skilled and motivated workers and substituted the criteria of minimal intelligence and amenability to routine. Not much more was required than the unimpaired use of arms and legs and the ability to understand simple commands.

The complexity and awkwardness of sixteenth-century firearms imposed a number of constraints on the system. The guns of that age were a far cry from today's automatic weapon with its two basic operations of inserting the cartridge and pulling the trigger. Muskets and calivers involved a multitude of steps: inserting powder, inserting bullet, ramming both, applying match, pulling trigger, etc.—all in all, forty-two. These took considerable time and under battlefield conditions were difficult to supervise in the mass.

It is characteristic of the Dutch that the guiding principles of their system were derived from the two most prominent components of the "new learning." The classical studies of William Louis complemented the mathematical interests of Maurice. The Roman technique of ordering soldiers in regularly spaced squares and rectangles and of altering the arrangement of lines by controlled maneuvers became practical when combined with a method for measuring output in quantitative terms.

The use of the countermarch shows the degree to which the Dutch system broke with the past in both ideology and technique. As a maneuver, the countermarch was as subversive as it was new. It violated the then cardinal principle of maintaining an unbroken mass at all costs. To allow soldiers to leave the front ranks was, in other armies, regarded as inviting them to panic and retreat.[34] That the Dutch could do so was a testimonial to the effectiveness of the new drill and to the capability of their officers.

The advantages of a military body of this kind were as much economical as tactical. It was the cheapest conceivable form of effective warfare, the one most amenable to a cost-effectiveness calculation. Dutch military practices provided a standard and a process for the regular manufacture of tactical units. The number of military variables was reduced to two: the availability of *raw* manpower, and the supply of manufactured weapons. The assembling of Spanish tercios, on the other hand, was dependent on the supply of indigenous manpower and on the imponderables governing the creation of the sense of solidarity and cohesion essential to the maintenance of a tight, unranked mass.

The Dutch reliance on articulated firepower rather than on massive cohesion rationalized military standards. Their units were basically interchangeable. Military proficiency could now be objectively measured. The drill system established criteria whereby a given number of men could be expected to get off a specific number of shots within a specific time. With both numbers and equipment standardized, it was simple to determine the effectiveness of units and to correct patent deficiencies. Each company represented a known productive capability. The state could therefore measure the cost of its maintenance against the resultant increase in manageable violence.

Military effectiveness could consequently be determined by criteria other than the elusive one of victory in battle. The quantification of firepower made command a technique for managing violence rather than an example of heroic leadership. Strategy in the Dutch style became the art of deploying soldiers under controlled working conditions, in positions where the rate of fire would be subject to the fewest encumbrances.

Although he commanded the Dutch forces for nearly forty years and the republic was at war for twenty-eight of them, Maurice fought only one pitched battle, and that unwillingly and under civilian pressure.[35] Otherwise, he campaigned like a chess master. He arranged soldiers so that their position, discipline, and firepower gave them an overwhelming local advantage. The probable price of battle was made too high. In view of this, the offensive-minded Spanish left him in command of the field.

III

Like the Nature of the old physics books, the Germans hated what they thought of as a pictorial vacuum, and believed that a good honest workman should fill his plate from corner to corner. If I may put the matter in philosophical jargon, even the greatest of them saw objects located in a space that was independent of them and unrelated to their forms, whereas the greater Italians saw that space was merely the relation between objects. If you see in this latter way, the spaces between objects become just as important as the objects themselves, for they are actually part of the objects, even possibly their most important part.[36]

The Dutch military revolution thus created of a mode of warfare that forged doctrine, weapons, and skills into a comprehensive system. It was revolutionary in that it was perhaps the first instance of machine technology's providing the basis for structuring a social organization. Discussions about which came first, Roman discipline or continuous firepower, are academic. [37] Discipline made continuous firepower possible and continuous firepower justified discipline. There is no evidence that an ordered pike formation would have offered any advantages over the massive conglomerates employed by the Spanish and the Swiss.

There is evidence of this in the history of the military reforms proposed by Machiavelli. Like the Dutch, Machiavelli saw in the revival of Roman legionary discipline a means of fabricating effective fighting units. He similarly believed that an externally imposed rational framework of formations and drill systems could compensate for the absence of a military tradition and transform an unwarlike population into combat units capable of resisting the communally bound Swiss and Spanish formations. [38]

In two major points, however, Machiavelli's proposals differed from the practices of the Dutch; the tactical relegation of firearms to a minimal role, [39] and the sociopolitical preference for a part-time militia force. [40] The first difference can be justified on tactical grounds. Machiavelli's Roman classical predilections were balanced by an equally strong aversion to contemporary military practices.

Dependence on infantry armed with firearms had by the late fifteenth century become a distinguishing characteristic of Italian armies. Firearms represented a technological breakthrough of which Italy, and especially Milan, the metallurgical workshop of Europe, was better prepared to take advantage than any other region. By 1476, one-fifth of the Milanese infantry were equipped with handguns. By the end of the century the proportion had become perhaps as high as one-third. [41]

This technological advance was not, however, a source of tactical superiority. The massive introduction of firearms coincided with the invasion of Italy by armies from societies which were both notably more backward and equipped and organized on a more traditional basis. The French, Swiss, and Spanish forces that humbled one Italian state after another still relied on heavily armored cavalry and on dense formation of pikemen and swordsmen.

The experience of Machiavelli's Italy indicated that reliance on firearms relaxed discipline and transformed infantry forces into bands of skirmishers. Whatever the technological advantages of this new instrument (in its admittedly crude stage of development), they did not compensate for the resultant loss of battlefield control. In proposing that the proportion of firearms be limited to a figure of approximately 5 per cent,[42] Machiavelli was not so much rejecting modernity as advocating the adoption of a military form that fitted the social and demographic characteristics of the late medieval city-state. A popular militia needed discipline more than anything else. That firearms and discipline were antithetical was a simple matter of contemporary observation. Moreover, for Machiavelli, a representative Renaissance Italian intellectual, steeped in the study of Latin literature, the legion was the instrument of discipline par excellence.

Machiavelli's second difference from the Dutch, his preference for a part-time militia force, was also a product of his practical experience and literary interests. In proposing that the new army be nonprofessional in both its enlisted men and officers,[43] Machiavelli was reacting to difficulties continually experienced by Florence and other Italian cities when waging war with mercenary armies. Dependence on hireling strangers had two probable consequences, each undesirable. The contracted commander avoided battle in order to draw out his salary for as long a period as possible and to keep the army, his stock in trade and capital, intact. If victorious, he would use his prestige and popularity to gain control of the contracting city. Machiavelli's anti-professionalism was also based on his familiarity with Roman history. He was well acquainted with the role played by successful generals and their long-term armies in the collapse of the late Roman Republic. The historical similarities of ancient Rome to fifteenth-century Italy were, for Machiavelli, so acute as to indicate a single solution to the problem that threatened both: the achievement of military security coupled with the avoidance of despotism. This solution was the retention, down to its very weaponry, of the legionary formation of the second century B.C.

There is, I suspect, yet another element in Machiavelli's preference for nonprofessional armies, namely, the intellectual's contempt for the military vocation. It is obvious that he thought the necessary skills in using pikes and swords were not very difficult to attain. His discussion of training emphasized toughening through physical exercises rather than the mastering of skills and routines. The military policy of the state should be directed toward ensuring for itself a sufficient quantity of able-bodied citizens, who were decidedly not to be trained as specialists in violence.[44] With the weapons he proposed, Machiavelli did not think that mechanical proficiency would make a decisive difference. He assumed that the outcome would be determined by the time-hallowed superiority of the legionary formation and by the sense of civic dedication and physical endurance intrinsic to it.

Machiavelli's military proposals, ironically enough, failed for reasons explicit in Roman history. Legionary experience did not guarantee an overwhelming collective sense of civic duty. Discipline, it turned out, was not so much a matter of ideological orientation as of military experience. The legionary formation was in and of itself not sufficient to create a cohesive force. The Spanish tercio routed the Florentine militia for much the same reason as it defeated the French and the pre-Maurician Dutch armies—not because of its superior armament, but because the armament was employed within a social system which succeeded in fusing the skills of its individual members into ingrained habits of group solidarity and operational cohesiveness. A prolonged record of victory transformed these habits into a tradition. Spanish soldiers were not necessarily more patriotic than their opponents and their officers were, by and large, not notably more intelligent. The tercio, however, was singularly imbued with a sense of its uniqueness as a social body. Its members fought, looted, and mutinied as a tightly bound, self-regulating unit. The sum of its parts seemed always to be greater than that of any of its rivals.[45]

Machiavelli and the Dutch shared, accordingly, three similar problems: creating an armed force that could stand up to the Spanish tercio, doing it in a way that would not undermine the civil institutions of their societies, and accomplishing this through adapting Roman military practices for contemporary usage. Where they differed was in their approach to possible solutions. For Machiavelli, it was a matter of ideology—the revival of the old Roman civic spirit.[46] For Maurice and his coworkers, it was a matter of technique—the development of procedures whereby rational design would cancel out the ingrained Spanish advantages of experience and tradition. For Maurice, the advantages of the Roman drill lay in the fact that it enabled him to use firearms in a controlled way. Roman drill gave him a system whereby the elementary skills of the available military manpower could be programmed toward a single desirable effect, the delivery of a competitively greater volume of missile shock. This system did not enhance the human or even the martial qualities of the individuals involved. Dutch armies were not noted for their valor, their élan, or their chivalry. They were simply dependable. The Florentine militia was a cottage industry. The Dutch army was a factory. (The Spanish tercio, a commune?)

The basis of Dutch military reforms is the fact that the Dutch army was organized around a body of officers specially trained to bring a rational approach to bear on the organization of masses of men for the production of violence. Its emphasis on drill and the use of firearms was ancillary to the creation of operational units that would be both self-sufficient and directly responsive to the technical skill of their managers. The two qualities were intimately related. The concept of an army composed of an assembly of autonomous units was the correlate of the concept of a body of officers unified by their adherence to a systematic body of technical knowledge. The concept of a professionally trained expert was fortified by a system that assigned him to units whose performance could be directly related to the application of his special managerial skills.

Apart from everything else, the success of the Dutch system was confirmed by imitation. The Dutch army rapidly became the school for a generation of Western European military officers. The Maurician reforms were the subject of many books published throughout Europe, especially in the Protestant areas.[47] Celebrated commanders like Gustavus Adolphus, Turenne, and Frederick William of Prussia were directly or indirectly educated in the Dutch army.[48] Service in the Dutch army became a conventional part of the education of the Western European gentry. The philosopher Descartes, attacted by Dutch religious tolerance and intellectual liveliness, settled in Holland. But what originally brought him there was, in the words of his earliest biographer, the desire to serve "as a volunteer (cadet) in the army of Prince Maurice, like many other of the younger sons of the French nobility who came to study the military profession under that great general." That lifelong student of rational, even mechanical, behavior in man was, in joining the Dutch army, especially animated by the wish "to study the various customs of man in their most natural state."[49]

In a broader sense, the Dutch military reforms can be credited with a major portion of responsibility for the spread of militarism and the rise of absolutism in seventeenth-century Europe. Armies created on the Dutch model increased the power of the sovereign to an unprecedented degree. They gave him exclusive use of the only industrialized system of the age. They made the conduct of war a monopoly of the central government, the agency with the largest and most regular flow of revenue. Feudal, peasant, and urban armed forces were driven out of competition. The national organization of war not only provided rulers with an overpowering instrument of coercion but also educated a body of military bureaucrats in the skills of penetrating into every level of society and of extracting its resources for their own particular objectives. This new capability was graphically manifested in France, Germany, Sweden, and Cromwellian England.[50] Yet here a praadox emerges. Dutch society, as already noted, remained the least militaristic, and Dutch government the least absolute, of all Western Europe. Inadvertently or otherwise, Maurice came closest to attaining the major objective of Machiavelli's military program— the creation of an army which, though effective, was not a threat to republican government.

The basis of this paradox is to be found in the peculiar history of the Dutch revolt and in the nature of the society it created. To enable the reader to grasp this point, I will present a compressed and necessarily narrow exposition of the general history of the Netherlands in the late sixteenth century.[51]

The Netherlands at the beginning of the revolt in 1568 was made up of seventeen provinces: ten to the south of the Rhine-Meuse-Scheldt river barrier, and seven to the north and within it. The barrier was not only geographic but economic and social as well. The southern provinces, present-day Belgium and northern France, were rolling, arable terrain. These provinces contained the prosperous farming areas, the seats of the higher nobility, the bulk of the episcopal seats, and the major commercial and industrial centers. The seven northern provinces, the present-day Netherlands, were sandy, waterlogged areas broken up by broad rivers, shallow lakes, and marshy stretches. They were sparsely cultivated and scantily populated, the local nobility were poor and scattered, and the ecclesiastical structure was weak. Their cities were largely in the two southern maritime provinces of Zeeland and Holland, and, with the significant exception of Amsterdam, they were relatively small and backward.

The revolt had its roots in two major policy objectives of Philip II, the Hapsburg ruler of Spain, Sicily, Naples, Milan, the Netherlands, most of the New World, etc. He wished to centralize the administration of his disparate and far-flung possessions in Madrid, his Spanish capital. His fervent Catholicism committed him to the personal mission of stamping out all heresy and religious dissidence not only within his own empire but also in all of Europe.

Two factors provided the necessary catalyst inciting the Dutch to revolt: their desire to maintain the original autonomy of the region, and their substantiated fear that tightened Spanish control would result in a violent repression of the widespread and growing Protestant sects. This combination of motives created an oddly joined front against the Hapsburg-appointed governors and their agents. On the one hand, the representatives of the great aristocratic families saw in Philip II's centralizing project a threat to their authority and privileges; on the other hand, the cities, primarily Antwerp, Bruges, Ghent, Valenciennes, Ypres, and Brussels, regarded the religious policies of the Spanish as a menace both to the free practice of their faith and to their traditional autonomy.

The revolt began as an urban-aristocratic coalition. In its opening phases it was waged largely in the southern provinces of the Netherlands, the area with large aristocratic estates and prosperous cities. The northern provinces were relatively quiescent.[52]

In its early stages, resistance to the monarch took the form of aristocratic discord and urban agitation. The aristocrats were, by and large, fighting to maintain the old order, the feudal autonomy of landed magnates. The cities were fighting for something new, the free and unhampered exercise of their religious beliefs. The unstable nature of this union was apparent from the beginning. The nobility were interested in maintaining an established tradition. The urban leaders were agents of religious change. In the southern cities, the cause of independence increasingly became identified with that of militant Calvinism, and incidentally with the desecration and spoliation of church property. The early success of the revolt tended to widen the division. To secure their control of the cities and to widen the basis of their support, the Calvinist leaders enlisted and armed the urban lower classes.

By 1578, these differences had created an open split. The higher nobility, alarmed by a movement which was growing beyond their original intentions and was now beginning to threaten their own interests and beliefs, began to come to terms with the Spanish regent. Forced to choose between acquiescence in the modernizing tendencies of an aristocratically based monarchy and participation in an urban revolt against their traditional religion and against the system of authority that was the basis of their status and wealth, they did what seemed natural to them. In increasing numbers, they reaffirmed their allegiance to both crown and church.

The split in the forces of revolution accelerated the process of aristocratic reconciliation. The Spanish were thus able to launch a counteroffensive. Their success had a twofold effect. In an effort to muster broader and more militant support, the urban leadership became increasingly Calvinist and popularist in nature. The landed faction saw both the objectives and leadership of the revolt passing out of their hands, and the middle and minor nobility found it easier to return to what they took to be the old system. The fact that the undisciplined and inexpertly led urban militias could not stand up to the regular Spanish forces confirmed them in this judgment. By 1585, what is now Belgium was almost entirely under Hapsburg control. The revolt had been crushed in its original seat.

The northern Netherlands, particularly the islands of Zeeland and the area bounded by the mouths of the Rhine, remained, however, unsubdued. There the river barriers, the marshy terrain, and the rebels' command of the sea and waterways encouraged resistance. But the very undeveloped nature of this region changed the character of the rebellion.

The Spanish reconquest of the southern Netherlands had forced a hard decision on its inhabitants: to come to terms with the conqueror or to continue the rebellion elsewhere. For the nobility, the choice was fairly easy. Conservatively inclined and alarmed by the radical tendencies of the cities, their status tied to the court and their estates largely in the occupied areas, they returned to the fold. By the same token, large numbers of the urban middle classes fled to the north. The Spanish occupation had not only proscribed their religion but had also destroyed the conditions of urban autonomy that were the foundation of commercial and industrial pursuits. In a way, exile was easier for the middle classes than for the aristocracy. The aristocracy's wealth lay in their landed possessions and official sinecures, both by nature nontransportable. Urban wealth was based on money and/or industrial and commercial skills. These could be and were transferred to the north.

Dutch society was thus polarized. The higher aristocracy and the organized Catholic clergy were concentrated in the south. The most radical and Calvinist of the middle and lower classes, and incidentally the most economically advanced, moved into the northwest corner, which they rapidly transformed into a religious, political, and economic bastion.

The original backwardness of the northern Netherlands facilitated this transformation. In the absence of a prominent local aristocracy[53] and of a strong ecclesiastical system, there were few local obstacles to Calvinist conversion. The destruction of the crown's authority enabled the cities to develop in full accord with their perceived economic and social interests. In the vacuum left by the elimination of bishops and nobles, the network of disciplined Calvinist consistories became the sole effective national system.[54] It made little difference that the members of the Reformed Church were, as late as 1587, a numerically insignificant fraction of the population.[55] Events had made Calvinism and independence virtually synonymous. The House of Orange-Nassau, the major noble family to remain with the revolt, had been almost driven to identify itself with both.

The Dutch thus became the first nonaristocratically governed modern European society. More significant for our purposes, they were the first modern state to be controlled by a class without a military tradition of its own. Maurice's army was created on this foundation. It was a mercenary force not so much by choice as by the nature of its political and social circumstances. The cluster of autonomous cities that dominated the Dutch Republic preferred supporting an army by regular monetary grants to having their social and economic structure continually disrupted by arbitrary and endless demands for military manpower. The insignificance of the northern Netherlands nobility and the underpopulation of the rural areas made it necessary to recruit most enlisted men and officers abroad.[56]

The army of the Dutch Republic was, in consequence, a new kind of armed force. It was the first national army without a corresponding social base. The modes of relationship that characterized the operations of the Dutch army were without analogues in the urban and the rural communities of the northern Netherlands. This is not to say that the army was free of the feudal aristocratic ethos prevalent in that age. Aristocratic military prejudices, however, had no social support. The commanding generals had a remarkably free hand in the organization of their forces. Their actions were subject to the approval only of the civilian commissioners who accompanied the army as representatives of States General.

The fact that the ordinary soldier was a salaried employee of the state rather than an adventurer not only made him more amenable to programmatic training and discipline but also expanded the concept of his duties to fit the commander's notions of military necessity. Until Maurice's time, for example, soldiers had considered using the spade for the preparation of field trenches as a task below their dignity. It was customary for armies to requisition local peasants for the labor of entrenchment and fortification. In the new Dutch army, the shovel was a standard part of the equipment of every infantryman.[57]

Similar factors facilitated the imposition of a rational command structure. Elsewhere, military subordination among officers was impeded by considerations of social status. Noblemen were likely to resent orders from anyone, especially people of a lower class.[58] In similar fashion, forms of military expertise that did not involve direct combat or in which competence was based on technical knowledge were looked down upon.[59] The engineering, artillery, and quartermaster branches were staffed by officers of nonnoble extraction. Their development and use betrayed the results of this attitude. The army of the Dutch Republic, on the other hand, was the first military force to place the employment of such branches on a systematic basis. Considerations of fortification, transport, and supply were the foundation of its operations.[60]

The army of the Netherlands can accordingly be cited as the earliest modern instance of a military culture, similar in scope to the factory cultures that sprang up in the Industrial Revolution. The behavior of its members was governed, to a notable degree, by the particular tools, language, and working habits imposed on them by the organizational system.[61] Until its emergence, armies had always mirrored the society from which they were drawn. Spanish armies operated in the style of the hidalgo, where impoverished men of honor acted in concert to defy their more lavishly endowed neighbors. Care was taken to enroll in the tercios a large number of gentlemen who served out of poverty and ambition and whose example would inspire the lower-born.[62] French armies were dominated by the spirit of the French aristocracy; their command structures mirrored the vicissitudes in power and fashion of the court hierarchy.[63] Machiavelli, as already noted, sought to establish an army which embodied republican virtues. The Dutch, in their unique way, created an army that would derive the maximum advantage from the available resources of men, money, and technology.

This earliest of industrial revolutions, the industrialization of military behavior in the Netherlands and consequently of political administration throughout Western Europe, was a reflection of Dutch political and social circumstances. "L'air bourgeois," La Rouchefoucauld (1613-1680) remarked, "se perd quelquefois à l'armée, mais il ne se perd jamas à la cour.[64] This was perhaps true in France. In the Netherlands, the situation was reversed. It could be said, "L'air noble se perd quelquefois à l'armée, mais il ne se perd jamais dans la ville." That is, "an aristocrat may pass unnoticed in the army, but in civil society he sticks out like a sore thumb." The trappings of nobility had a scanty or even a negative role in the Dutch distributive scheme of social, political, and economic rewards.[65]

For the period under discussion, what there was of a Dutch court was at The Hague, the official residence of the Orange family. It was far from being the focus of national life. Maurice of Nassau, although the most powerful, was not the most influential national figure. He had few apparent dynastic ambitions.[66] He did little to establish a network of urban allegiances that might have transformed his power into a conduit for the distribution of office and wealth. His palace at The Hague was the core of an overgrown village, opposed in its tastes and manners to the ideology of the urban oligarchy which dominated Dutch society.

Though of independent pricely rank, Maurice was not a reigning monarch. His authority was personal and had neither a political nor an administrative apparatus to back it up. This had a peculiar effect on the social role of the Dutch army. Officers were imprisoned within a system of grades that was strictly functional. Achievement could not, as in other societies, be rewarded with enoblement or with a higher title. Maurice did not have at his disposal that reservoir of public lands and offices which contemporary monarchs distributed as tokens of their favor and approval. There was, consequently, no apparatus for bringing military distinction into correspondence with political and social status.[67] For the meager Dutch aristocracy, therefore, military careers represented a substitute for the larger political and social arenas in which they could not compete.

All this is a reflection of the peculiar relationship that existed between the periphery and the center in the northern Netherlands. The dominant cities, Amsterdam in particular, disassociated themselves from the national governing apparatus. Their regents preferred to concentrate their political energies on the active control of the municpal posts which, by virtue of their being the key instruments of economic policy, were the real seats of power. Dutch oligarchs participated in the national governments through the device of rigidly controlled delegates who were generally of a distinctly inferior social level.[68] The control of national policy was thus in the hands of a group of individuals who deliberately limited their personal involvement in politics to the management of local and private interests. This served their interests well. The national agencies had, at best, a nominal authority. The House of Orange could, if it wished, dominate them. But so long as it was excluded from the system of urban offices, its intervention could have little effect.

The Dutch military officer was, accordingly, preeminently a technocrat. He had neither the status nor the tradition to make his very presence the focal point of society and the model of social behavior. The position he had occupied, both literally and figuratively, on the battlefield was notable, not for the treasure of military and personal virtues contained in his person, but for the network of functional obligations which passed through it. His role depended not so much on what he was assumed to be as on what he was obliged to know.[69]

This development is similar in concept, if not in importance, to the Renaissance discovery of linear perspective. Earlier armies had been dominated by a system of established social relationships. They were ordered according to a simple disjunctive scale of statused and nonstatused individuals. The distance between noble officers and common enlisted men was qualitatively so great as to preclude any schematic rendering. The distinction between aristocrat and lowborn was so intrinsic and so fundamental as to make the actual interval which separated one individual from another relatively unimportant.[70] It was a contrast between one class, the nobility, who led because they enjoyed an innate monopoly of the highest of all virtues, the martial ones, and another, the enlisted men, who served because nothing at all positive could be expected of them.[71]

Following this principle, armed units operated in the densest mass possible, the lower orders imitating and reinforcing the behavior of the leaders. The density of each unit corresponded to the status of its commander. Its military proficiency depended on its ability to maintain this connection—present a single face, so to speak.

The Dutch system, on the other hand, created a positive and detailed expectation about the role of each individual soldier. It therefore required a spatial and operational framework by virtue of which the role performance could be supervised and controlled. The relationship between officers and enlisted men was thus reciprocal. Command involved not only the responsibility for one's personal post but also the systematic supervision of subordinates. Subordination entailed not merely responsiveness to the superior's commands but also execution in accordance with a fixed and common procedure. Rank was determined not by an ability to coalesce members into an undifferentiated mass but according to detailed responsibility, i.e., the number of specialized individuals and fixed relationships for which the officer was responsible. The maintenance of such relationships was as important as the officer's presence on the battlefield. More so—the spatial, and not the status, pattern made it possible to manipulate firearms as part of a controlled system. It made it possible for tactical units to evolve within the system of a "full cycle," and to achieve their objective of a continuous rate of fire.

IV

The principles of warfare embodied in the Maurician reforms have been generally criticized on two counts. The rigid insistence on organizational space made the Dutch forces stiff and unwieldly and, therefore, unsuited to offensive operations. Since the pattern was predominant, infantry organized on the Dutch principles could not deliver a mass charge or win pitched battles. The emphasis on the maintenance of fixed intervals, moreover, limited their application of the Maurician principles to the open terrain characteristic of the Netherlands. In heavily wooded and broken areas, the Dutch were at a distinct disadvantage.[72] In the second place, mercenary armies on the Dutch model were expensive. The problem of providing regular pay for field armies either seriously limited both the length and nature of campaigns or drained the economic resources of the state.[73]

The historian Michael Roberts, whose authority is not to be lightly disputed, sees in Gustavus Adolphus of Sweden the heir and perfector of the Maurician system. Gustavus Adolphus modified the Dutch tactical unit and adapted it for offensive operations. The principle of continuous fire was replaced by that of missile shock, that is, a salvo delivered by two ranks at a time. The number of pikemen was increased. This plus the development of a standardized mobile artillery reintroduced the massed infantry charge. In addition, he introduced the principle of military conscription in Sweden and established the first truly national army.[74]

Roberts's argument, it seems to me, ignores two distinct but related facts. The Swedish army, like the Spanish army before it, achieved many victories. But none of them was decisive. In pursuit of the elusive goal of victory, manpower resources were exhausted and the treasury drained. Second, the Swedish mode of warfare was cheap, not because it was national, but because it was successful. It was supported by the loot of conquered areas (*bellum se ipsum alet*). But as the theater of war was repeatedly devastated, exactions diminished. The relentless pursuit of victory was decisive only in its social and economic havoc. The ancillary policy of paying soldiers with national revenue assignments or of allotting farms to them depressed and eventually overwhelmed the Swedish economy.[75]

Maurice had the advantage of operating within the social and political framework of a middle-class republic. The preeminence of the urban oligarchs had the unique effect of making the economic sphere dominant over the military sphere. Everywhere else it was the other way around. At the end of the Eighty Year War, the United Provinces of the Netherlands were markedly more populous and more prosperous than they had been at the beginning.

Maurice's military objective was not to defeat his opponent but to wear him down. The division of Dutch wartime management into distinct civil and military spheres made this objective feasible. The commander of the armed forces was responsible not for gaining victories but for keeping his armies undefeated and efficient; efficient meant operating close to their full firepower capacity. The States General had the responsibility of seeing that the military were regularly paid and supplied. This they did with remarkable regularity, not because the Dutch middle classes had a genius for making money but because they and the society they headed were able to devote themselves to that activity in a single-minded and unimpeded way.

With his forces regularly paid, Maurice could afford to avoid pitched battles and wait for the predictable spells of Spanish exhaustion. In such intervals, he would pry one territorial objective after another from Spanish grasp. Concentration on the practices of fortification, entrenchment, and controlled defensive fire kept Maurice's forces in a condition where battle was always too expensive for his opponents.

The fact that the Dutch system of warfare was not designed for widespread application cannot be validly criticized. It was not meant to be an instrument of hegemony. The perceived European interests of the Dutch Republic were pursued by means more of the purse than of the sword. The genius of the Maurician system lay in its unique adaptation to the nature and objectives of the Dutch revolt. It sought to create an effective army for a middle-class republic without distorting the constitutional framework or the social composition of the setting where it operated. After 1585, the Dutch Republic existed to defend the autonomy of its component parts and to promote the industrial and commercial interests of their inhabitants.

This was, perhaps, a narrow view; and the United Provinces have been criticized for it. Their expansive aspirations were directed toward creating an overseas empire. In Europe, they showed no desire to expand beyond the frontiers that had been traditionally theirs. The acquisition of an extensive hinterland could only have created new enemies and increased the burden of military support.

The attribution of intellectual parenthood for the Dutch military reforms to the Netherlands' classicist and neo-Stoic philosopher, Justus Lipsius (1547-1606), is another instance of the tendency to place the Dutch military experience in a broader context. The case for Lipsius is impressive but circumstantial. He was a professor at the University of Leiden and taught Maurice of Nassau. He wrote extensively about the reformation of politics, morals, and warfare according to the model of Roman theory and practice. Two of his books, *De militia Romana libri quinque* and *Politicorum sive civilis doctrinae libri sex,* are in the inventory of Prince Maurice's library. His books were, throughout the seventeenth century, the most widely translated and reprinted European philosophical works.[76]

It is incontestable that Lipsius played a major role in the reaffirmation of Roman discipline and military practices as the instrument of military reform. He clearly influenced Maurice's thought and outlook. The case for his being the originator rests, however, on shaky grounds. As Michael Roberts has remarked, "the tactical maxims of Vegetius and Aelian were commonplaces to the military writers of the age."[77] But their adaptation to the deployment of firearms and the attainment of continuous fire belongs to Maurice and his cousin William Louis.

The attribution of parenthood to Lipsius, moreover, is based on cultural generalities. In actuality, there were significant differences between Dutch practice and the policies advocated by the neo-Stoic philosopher. The model of military and political perfection conceived by Lipsius envisaged a state where the ruler had absolute authority, where the army was a national militia, and where the basic military virtues of prudence, justice, fortitude, and temperance were regarded as the foundation of civic education. Lipsius recommended Roman discipline as a means of achieving moral uplift through continuous drill. It was a device whereby the prince would transfer his own exemplary military, religious, and ethical qualities to the people he ruled.[78] The contemporary ruler most influenced by Lipsius was Maximilian I of Bavaria (1573-1651). In military matters, he was a thoroughgoing conservative and a textbook follower of the Belgian philosopher. In the political realm, equally influenced by Lipsius, he as a proto-absolutist.[79] The Dutch state, on the other hand, was strikingly nonabsolutist. Political pluralism was, in its case, balanced by military pragmatism. Its army was a mercenary force, unified neither by nationality nor by religion. Its military system operated in an atmosphere of moral neutrality. In contrast to the Spanish, Swedish, and Cromwellian armies, the Dutch made no provision for chaplains in the company table of organization.

The particularist nature of Dutch military doctrine was the basis of its experimental and improvising approach. The army was not the prime instrument of national policy; commerce filled that role. Military activity along the land frontiers of the Netherlands played a part analogous to the dikes and drainage works along the seacoast. It was designed to ward off catastrophe and provide a secure environment for profitable investment. An effective army, like an effective polderman, was one that maximized the routine dependability of the system and minimized the cost of its maintenance.

This auxiliary capacity turned out, strangely enough, to be a source of strength. The army was effectively shielded both from the prevalent aristocratic military ethic and from the political and religious ideological extremes of the conflict. Its tactics and operations were made to conform to externally imposed criteria and its personnel were recruited largely for technical competence and competitive market price. The presence of whole regiments of Catholics was not a rarity. It is no accident that Maurice, a champion of international Calvinism, had as his most trusted technical expert Simon Stevin, a lifelong Catholic. It is noteworthy that Lipsius was horrified by the idea of religious diversity and toleration in a state; the Dutch acceptance of them drove him back to Belgium and his original Catholic faith.[80]

The most innovative military contribution of the Dutch Republic may well have been that it was dominated by the middle class. This was the basis of its sharp, novel differentiation between the civil and the military spheres. The entailed principles imposed limits on its conduct of war. Matters of broad policy and strategy were decided by nonmilitary leaders. Technical proficiency and logistical responsibility were the preoccupation of military commanders. The middle-class control of the United Provinces, moreover, meant that the class with political power was also devoid of military ambitions. With the very significant exception of the House of Orange-Nassau, the aristocracy were in no position to use the army as a bulwark of their privileges or to exploit it as an instrument of their policies. The army that created the Dutch Republic was conducted as if it were an indispensable but burdensome form of insurance. It embodied the actuarial principle of limiting losses in order to consolidate gains.

NOTES

1. K. W. Swart, "The Miracle of the Dutch Republic as Seen in the Seventeenth Century," an inaugural lecture delivered at the University College, London, 6 November 1967; published for the college by H. K. Lewis & Co. (London: n.d.); also E. H. Kossman, *In Praise of the Dutch Republic: Some Seventeenth Century Attitudes* (London: University College, 1963). The best short survey in English is J. H. Huizinga, "Dutch Civilization in the Seventeenth Century," in Huizinga, *Dutch Civilization in the Seventeenth Century and Other Essays,* selected by Pieter Geyl and F.W.N. Hugenholtz, trans. Arnold J. Pomerans (New York: Harper Torchbooks, 1968). An indispensable guide is provided by Pieter Geyl in his three books on the period: *The Revolt of the Netherlands (1555-1609)* (London: Benn, 1958); and *The Netherlands in the Seventeenth Century,* Vol. 1, *1609-1648;* Vol. 2, *1648-1715* (London: Benn, 1961). A useful survey of the social and cultural background is J. L. Price, *Culture and Society in the Dutch Republic during the Seventeenth Century* (London: Batsford, 1974).

2. Joseph R. Stayer, *On the Medieval Origins of the Modern State* (Princeton, N.J.: Princeton University Press, 1970), p. 5.

3. K.H.D. Haley, *The Dutch in the Seventeenth Century* (New York: Harcourt Brace Jovanovich, 1972), p. 71.

4. Huizinga, "Dutch Civilization," pp. 36 ff.; see also Werner Hahlweg, *Die Heeresreform der Oranier and die Antike* (Berlin: Junker & Dünnhaupt, 1941), p. 20.

5. Sir William Temple, *Observations upon the United Provinces of the Netherlands (1673),* ed. Sir George Clark (Oxford: Clarendon Press, 1972), p. 52.

6. Huizinga, "Dutch Civilization," p. 34.

7. Sir John Davies, "Orchestra, or a Poem on Dancing," in *Silver Poets of the Sixteenth Century,* ed. Gerald Bullett (New York: Everyman's Library, 1949), p. 338.

8. Geyl, *Revolt,* p. 219.

9. Jelle C. Riemersma, *Religious Factors in Early Dutch Capitalism 1550-1650* (The Hague: Mouton, 1967), p. 31.

10. Jan Willem Wijn, *Het Krijgswezen in den Tijd vans Prins Maurits* (Utrecht: Drukkerij Hoeijenbos & Co., 1934), pp. 28-29.

11. Ibid, pp. 120-24; also Jan Den Tex, *Oldenbarnevelt,* trans. R. B. Powell, 2 vols. (Cambridge: At the University Press, 1973), 1:124, 280.

12. Geoffrey Parker, *The Army of Flanders and the Spanish Road 1567-1659* (Cambridge: At the University Press, 1972), pp. 185 ff.; also Charles Wilson, *Queen Elizabeth and the Revolt of the Netherlands* (Berkeley: University of California Press, 1970), p. 13; Leon van der Essen, *Alexandre Farnèse, Prince de Parme Gouverneur Général des Pays-Bas (1545-1592),* with a preface by Henri Pirenne (Brussels: Librairie Nationale d'Art et d'Histoire, 1934), 2: 52-56.

13. Parker, *Army of Flanders,* pp. 40-41.

14. Fritz Redlich, *De Praeda Militari: Looting and Booty, 1500-1815* (Wiesbaden: Franz Steiner, 1956), pp. 2-5.

15. Parker, *Army of Flanders,* p. 185.

16. The polyarchic nature of the Dutch confederacy was an essential component of its financial structure. The monetary resources of the traditional monarchies were derived from two sources: the royal demense and extraordinary grants from the kingdom's component Estates. These were spent in an unbudgeted fashion according to the monarch's needs and desires. Any surplus was retained for his own use. The

States General of the Dutch Republic had neither such means nor such powers. Sovereignty was vested in the individual provinces or, more precisely, in their incorporated municipalities. The latter, in effect, paid an annual rent to the central government for the use of its special services, i.e., its army and navy. The rise of the absolute state can, in financial terms, be described as an arrogation by the latter of the fiscal powers of its formerly autonomous Estates and municipalities. Cf. F. L. Carsten, *Princes and Parliaments in Germany: From the Fifteenth to the Eighteenth Century* (Oxford: Claredon Press, 1959).

17. There is an excellent modern facisimile edition–Jacob de Gheyn, *The Exercise of Armes,* with commentary by J. B. Kist (New York: McGraw-Hill, 1971).

18. Carl A. Thimm, *A Complete Bibliography of Fencing and Duelling, as Practiced by All European Nations from the Middle Ages to the Present Day* (London: John Lane, 1896), esp. pp. 392-417. It is curious that he includes de Gheyn as the first Dutch fencing manual.

19. William M. Ivins, Jr., *Prints and Visual Communication* (Cambridge: Harvard University Press, 1953), p. 16.

20. Books of dance instruction may have been published even before fencing manuals. The earliest known example is ca. 1490; see Michel Toulouze, *L'Art et Instruction de Bien Dancer,* a facsimile with a bibliographical note by Victor Scholderer (London: Royal College of Physicians, 1936).

21. The first schools of arms arose among the middle classes. They were designed to provide by conscientious application what the upper classes possessed by virtue of their traditions and style of life. Endurance was the prime quality of knightly prowess. The lower classes relied on skill. See Egerton Castle, *Schools and Masters of Fencing,* with a foreward by R. A. Lidstone, 3d ed. (London: Arms & Armour Press, 1969), pp. 13-14, 34-43.

22. There is a striking resemblance between this and a Wittgensteinian language game; see Ludwig Wittgenstein, *Philosophical Investigations* (Oxford: Blackwell, 1958), Part I: 2, 8, esp. 19. "It is easy to imagine a language consisting only of orders and reports in battle." It also seems to contradict some of the precepts of structural linguistics: "Any grammar of a language will project the finite and somewhat accidental corpus of observed utterances to a set (presumably infinite) of grammatical utterances" (Noam Chomsky, *Syntatic Structures* [The Hague: Mouton, 1962], p. 15). The corpus of observed military utterances is in this case finite and *nonaccidental.* Moreover, one can imagine a comprehensive martinet system which covers every possible–i.e., permitted–act and admits of no extension. This perhaps provides us with a clue for the manner in which military social systems differ from other social modes.

23. Hahlweg, *Heeresreform,* pp. 233 ff. This also may have been independently anticipated in handbooks of dance. One of the most popular, Thoinot Arbeau, *Orchesography* (1589), trans. Mary Steward Evans, with introduction and notes by Julia Sutton (New York: Dover, 1967), presents the notion of a full cycle (p. 112). The steps, however, are not illustrated in serial order but referred to parallel to the musical notation. It incidentally mentions the Roman military author, Tacticus, as providing an example of how music can be used in developing cadenced military marching (p. 37).

24. Ivins, *Prints,* pp. 16-17, fixes the first industrial application of this method in Joseph Moxon's *Mechanick Exercises* 1683).

25. Kist, *Commentary on de Gheyn,* p. 14.

26. Ludwig Plathner, "Graf Johann von Nassau und die erste Kreigschule" (Inaugural dissertation, Friedrich-Wilhelms-Universität zu Berlin, 1913), pp. 15 ff.

27. Kist, *Commentary on de Gheyn*, p. 6; also D. J. Dijksterhuis, *Simon Stevin* (The Hague: Martinus Nijhoff, 1943), pp. 321-332.

28. Kist, *Commentary on de Gheyn*, p. 7; also Hahlweg, *Heeresreform*, p. 197 ff. Sixteenth-century editors as well as Kist and Hahlweg attribute the work in question to one Claudius Aelian. The proper author, however, seems to be an equally shadowy Greek, Aelian Tacticus; see K. K. Müller, "Aelianus," *Real-Encyclopädie der Classischen Altertumswissenschaft*, Vol. I (Stuttgart: Pauly-Wissowa, 1894), 1: 482-486.

29. Hahlweg, *Heeresreform*, pp. 279-285.

30. Parker, *Army of Flanders*, p. 274.

31. F.J.G. Ten Raa and F. De Bas, *Het Staatsche Leger* (Breda: De Koninklijke Militaire Academie, 1913), 2: 332-335.

32. The Spanish roster included a page and a chaplain as officers. The Dutch significantly had no chaplains at the company level and treated the pages as supernumeraries. If the page and chaplain are subtracted from the Spanish totals, the officer totals become 143 and 54—a ratio of better than 2.6:1 in favor of the Dutch.

33. Ten Raa and De Bas, *Staatsche Leger*, p. 335; Kist, *Commentary on de Gheyn*, p. 7.

34. Sir Charles Oman, *A History of the Art of War in the Sixteenth Century* (New York: Dutton, n.d.), p. 70.

35. Geyl, *Revolt*, p. 244

36. Ivins, *Prints*, p. 64.

37. Max Weber, *From Max Weber: Essays in Sociology,* trans. and ed. H. H. Gerth and C. Wright Mills (New York: Oxford University Press, 1946), pp. 256-257; also David Rapoport, "Military and Civil Societies: The Contemporary Significance of a Traditional Subject in Political Theory," Political Studies 12 (June 1964): 178-201.

38. Niccolo Machiavelli, *The Art of War,* trans. Ellis Franesworth, rev. with an introduction by Neal Wood (Indianapolis: Bobbs-Merrill, 1965), p. 209.

39. Ibid., pp. 61-62.

40. Ibid., pp. 28 ff.

41. Michael Mallett, *Mercenaries and Their Masters* (Totowa, N.J.: Rowmann & Littlefield, 1974), pp. 157 ff.

42. Machiavelli, *Art of War*, pp. 61.

43. Ibid., pp. 17 ff.

44. Ibid., pp. 57 ff.

45. Parker, *Army of Flanders*, pp. 32, 185-206.

46. "Machiavelli had hoped that by increasing and developing military organization, the hegemony of the city over the countryside could be created, and for this reason can be called the first Italian Jacobin." In Antonio Gramsci, *Letters from Prison*, trans., comp., and intro. Lynne Lawner (New York: Harper & Row, 1973), p. 205.

47. Kist, *Commentary on de Gheyn*, pp. 18-27.

48. Michael Roberts, "Gustav Adolph and the Art of War," in *Essays in Swedish History* (Minneapolis: University of Minnesota Press, 1967), p. 63; A. M. Ramsay, *Histoire du Vicomte de Turenne,* 2 vols. (Paris: Chez la Veuve Mazières J. B. Garnier, 1735), 1: 7-16; Ferdinand Schevill, *The Great Elector* (Chicago: University of Chicago Press, 1947), pp. 81-83.

49. Adrien Bailet, *Vie de Monsieur Descartes (1691)* (Paris: La Table Ronde, 1946), pp. 23 ff. Descartes, who remained a Catholic, had a lifelong interest in the problem of automatons, See also Geyl, *Revolt*, p. 244.

50. Roberts, "The Military Revolution 1560-1660," in *Essays,* pp. 200-208.
51. Geyl, *Revolt,* passim.
52. Ibid., pp. 79 ff.
53. Ibid., pp. 131 ff.; Jan de Vries, *The Dutch Rural Economy in the Golden Age, 1500-1800* (New Haven: Yale University Press, 1974), p. 35. The accredited noble class of sixteenth-century Holland included no more than twelve families. By the eighteenth century, their number had been reduced to six.
54. H. G. Koenigsberger, "The Organization of Revolutionary Parties in France and the Netherlands during the 16th Century," in *Estates and Revolutions* (Ithaca, N.Y.: Cornell University Press, 1971), pp. 234-242.
55. Geyl, *Revolt,* p. 131. At that date they were estimated to be one-tenth of the population of Holland, the chief province of the rebellious area.
56. Temple, *Observations,* p. 128.
57. Wilson, *Queen Elizabeth,* p. 111.
58. Hans Speier, "Militarism in the 18th Century," in *Social Order and the Risks of War* (Cambridge: MIT Press, 1969), p. 232.
59. F. L. Carsten, *The Origins of Prussia* (Oxford: Clarendon Press, 1954), p. 271.
60. Wijn, *Krijgswezen,* pp. 319-328, 376-388.
61. Claude Lévi-Strauss, "Linguistics and Anthropology," in *Structural Anthropology* (Garden City, N.Y.: Doubleday Anchor, 1967), pp. 66 ff.
62. Parker, *Army of Flanders,* pp. 40-41.
63. Speier, "Militarism," p. 234.
64. La Rochefoucauld, *Oeuvres Complètes* (Paris: Bibliothèque de la Pléiade, 1950), p. 302.
65. Peter Burke, *Venice and Amsterdam: A Study of Seventeenth Century Elites* (London: Temple Smith, 1974), passim.
66. His case is somewhat complicated. Maurice was not the titular head of his house. He never married. His elder brother, Philip William (1554-1618), a captive in Spain from 1568 on and a Catholic, did not return to the Netherlands until the truce of 1609. It is noteworthy that Maurice did not turn against the civil leader Oldenbarnevelt and make himself the dominant figure in the state until his older brother had died. His successful leadership did, however, bring about a steady increase in the family fortunes. William the Silent was addressed as "Your Excellency." His third son, Frederick Henry, Maurice's successor, with victory assured in 1635, gained the title "Your Highness." Frederick Henry's son, William II, unsuccessfully tried for royal status. His grandson, William III, more or less achieved it.
67. Price, *Culture and Society,* pp. 58-61.
68. Ibid, pp. 67-68.
69. See chapter 3, this book.
70. It is generally agreed that both in primitive art and in the reviving naturalism of the period leading up to the Renaissance, an interest in the object itself preceded any interest in space as such. The interval, or nothingness, which separates one solid from the next, is relatively unimportant. See John White, *The Birth and Rebirth of Pictoral Space* (New York: Harper & Row, Icon Editions, 1972), p. 35.
71. Speier, "Militarism," p. 235.
72. Roberts, *Essays,* pp. 61 ff.
73. Ibid., pp. 199 ff.
74. Ibid., pp. 64-66.
75. Ibid., pp. 227-228.

76. Gerhard Oestreich, "Justus Lipsius als Teoretiker des neuzeitlicher Machstaates," in *Geist und Gestalt des frühmodernen Staates* (Berlin: Duncker & Humblot, 1969), pp. 37 ff.; Kist, *Commentary on de Gheyn,* p. 10.
77. Roberts, *Essays,* p. 60.
78. Oestreich, "Der römische Stoizismus und die oranische Heeresreform," in *Geist und Gestalt,* pp. 19 ff.
79. Dollinger, Heinz, "Kufürst Maximilian I. Von Bayern und Justus Lipsius," Archiv fur Kultur geschichte, 1964, Band XLVI, Heft 213: 227-308, esp. pp. 282 ff.
80. Oestreich, "Justus Lipsius in sua re," in *Geist und Gestalt,* pp. 94 ff.

ABOUT THE AUTHOR

MAURY FELD is a historian and sociologist who has specialized in the study of the military profession and military organization. He is the librarian at the Center for International Affairs, Harvard University. He is also the book review editor of the journal *Armed Forces and Society* and has contributed numerous articles and reviews to scholarly and professional journals.